Appalachian Daug[hters]

The Exodus of the Mountainee[rs from] Appalachia

Helen Ayers

Bloomington, IN  Milton Keynes, UK

AuthorHouse™
1663 Liberty Drive, Suite 200
Bloomington, IN 47403
www.authorhouse.com
Phone: 1-800-839-8640

AuthorHouse™ UK Ltd.
500 Avebury Boulevard
Central Milton Keynes, MK9 2BE
www.authorhouse.co.uk
Phone: 08001974150

© 2006 Helen Ayers. All rights reserved.

No part of this book may be reproduced, stored in a retrieval system, or transmitted by any means without the written permission of the author.

First published by AuthorHouse 4/6/2006

ISBN: 1-4259-1657-0 (sc)

Printed in the United States of America
Bloomington, Indiana

This book is printed on acid-free paper.

Foreword

I started writing this book two years ago to preserve family stories and lore for our two sons and two grandchildren. Throughout the book I attempt to weave the strands of love for home, church and family apparent throughout my stories and how that love and strength was passed down from generation to generation. The strength of the women in the stories more than match that of their male counterparts.

When my brothers and sisters heard of my efforts they wanted stories in the book about themselves, so I added those because they helped me tell a more complete story. As I started putting my stories together into book form other ideas intruded and I somehow started writing about the entire group of people who left the Appalachian Mountain area about the same time my family did. I could not tell the story of our family without also telling of the influence the others had on the exodus, so it grew into the following book.

I know each of my siblings and the others I speak about might remember things differently than I have explained them. This is simply because each of us views the same events with different eyes. The stories I am relating here are best described as factual fiction. Because of my very young age (6) when we left the mountains I cannot remember the exact words we used to each other of course, but I recall the events vividly.

The book attempts to describe the impact our departure had on the areas we moved to as well as on the area we left behind. When I use the terms "our" and "we" now I am speaking of not just my family, but for all these other families as well.

This story has been begging to be told for half a century. I kept expecting someone else to write about the exodus of the mountaineers from Appalachia, but no one did. Placing my fingers on my keyboard, I finally decided to write the story myself.

Thanks

It would not have been possible to write a book like this without the assistance and contributions of many others who became involved as I wrote and started assembling the stories into book form. The oldest memories I have are those of a very young girl since we moved to Indiana when I was only six years old. They continue on and encompass three generations.

First of all I would like to thank my sisters Sylvia Ziegler and Anna Mikels who provided me with several pictures and much encouragement; our sons Lonnie and Doug Ayers for their chapter ideas and for keeping me focused on the project; my young artist friend Frank Fisher for his rendition of an old truck on the last page; the neighborhood computer guru, Tom Stoebick; and especially Theresa Osborne who supplied all the archive mining pictures I used in the book. The mining pictures are used with permission from The Benham Lynch Collection of the Southeast Kentucky Community and Technical College Appalachian Archive, Cumberland, KY. One of them was used as my book cover. Also the many people at Authorhouse who helped make this book a reality. The influence of many others is accepted and I am thankful. It is just hard to remember everyone who has provided encouragement to me, but I thank them too.

And, lastly, I want to thank my soul mate, my husband, Mickey, for washing the dishes and cleaning the floors and stuff like that to give me time to write the book. And all the people in my past who lived the same life I did for awhile and who left me these memories.

Our Cover Photographs

The small picture is one of the author when she was five years old in the first grade of Cowan School in Eastern Kentucky.

The picture of the old truck coming down the mountain through a series of "S" curves is one of the Wainscot photos in the archives of the Southeast Kentucky Community and Technical College Appalachian Archive in Cumberland, Ky. (Used by Permission.)

Table of Contents

Foreword v
Thanks vii

The Decision to Move 1
Goodbye to Cowan Creek 10
   Aunt Anita's square dance calls: *14*
   The Maypole Song and Dance *16*
Those Left Behind 20
Uncle Ned 25
Mother and the Church 30
The Two-Room School 41
The Kitchen Table 49
The Easter Parade 58
The Family Community 62
My Turn at Motherhood 71
Hobos and the Train 80
Three Witches 86
The Turkey 92
Summertime Chores 98
Tadpoles, Snakes and Pearls 112
Sister Annie 117
The Haystacks 122
Pie Suppers, Quilts and Aprons 125

Curtain Stretchers 132
The Welfare Solution 136
Sylvia's Drowning 143
House Building... 147
Ain't Love Grand... 154
    Lolly-Gagging... *161*
Learning to Drive.. 162
Grandma's Redneck School of Driving 166
Those Lying Hound Dogs 173
Those Awful Ragweeds 179
Suckers and Mushrooms 185
Cooking Like a Kentuckian... 193
Grapevine Swings 195
Mick and TNT 203
Final Goodbyes... 207
    Misty Jane.. *217*
Farewell 218
Precious Memories Recitation 219

Wainscott Hillside Farm

The Decision to Move

The Depression years were now behind them, World War II had ended and the soldiers had come home. We knew it had ended when we heard a great racket coming up Cowan Creek in the mountains of Eastern Kentucky sometime in the middle of 1945. What we had heard was a band of young men and women in the bed of an old truck, beating on washtubs and other noise makers, shouting, "The war is over, the war is over" as they were driven up and down first one road and another. Not many people had radios then and this was the way the war news was spread.

But with the war over, another great upheaval was on the horizon as the migration of the residents from the coalfields of Eastern Kentucky to the land of plenty to the north was just beginning.

Many decades earlier a similar migration had taken place. The residents of the Pine Mountain area of Eastern Kentucky had left their homes along the eastern coastal states of the United States and followed explorer Daniel Boone through the Cumberland Gap into the wilds of beautiful Kentucky. Those early families, mine included, decided to settle in the valleys and heavily forested mountains of Eastern Kentucky. Most of the settlers in this area were of English and Irish extraction. They had already left their country of origin behind and settled on the eastern costal states. Then Mr. Boone tempted them to move once again. Here they would scratch for their livelihoods growing small patches of vegetables and fruits for their own daily fare and corn for feed for their one or two horses or mules and a cow and some pigs and chickens. They made a pretty good living hewing the virgin timber stands, then floating the logs to Frankfort and selling them.

The virgin timber they cut would be marked with their personal identification and tied into rafts during fall and winter on the Kentucky River that meandered crookedly from town to town for hundreds of miles. Once the spring floods came, the flotilla of saw logs would be floated to Frankfort, the capital of Kentucky, and there sold to timber buyers. Our own "Pap" Caudill, our Mother's dad Jesse, would actually live on those "rafts" for many days until his log rafts reached the log market in Frankfort.

Once the timber was sold Pap would then walk or hop a freight train back to the mountains and start to repeat the process. The land was cleared in this manner, providing an income, firewood for their own use and making the ground available for planting more crops. I have seen pictures of tall men standing at the butt of one of the saw logs and the puny humans looked like midgets standing before them the logs were so thick at the base. Our maternal grandmother, Mary "Mama" Miller Caudill, used to entertain us with stories of her husband's trips down the river taking these logs to market.

Some of the mountain migrants of the middle to late 1940s went with their families to Detroit, Chicago and Cincinnati to seek jobs in the newly revamped factories now retooled from the war effort and turned to post-war production. Americans were sick and tired of the war and wanted many things that had become scarce during the war. The jobs these migrants were given paid well and provided a very good living for those families. They came from such colorful place names in the mountains as Cowan, King's Creek, Kingdom Come, Whitesburg, Day, Ice, Line Fork and Dongola, Kentucky.

Several of those migrants, including ours, came not to the factories in the cities of the north, but to the gently rolling terrain of Jackson County, Indiana. Some of them would become farmers on the fertile land, while a large number became highly skilled union carpenters in Columbus and Seymour. Most would always work in a supervisory capacity because they had such a strong and dependable work ethic and knew how to lead other men. While living in Kentucky, they had been considered the "cream of the crop." They never missed a day of work unless they were just absolutely too sick to work so they could always be depended upon to show up on the job site.

They were a proud hard-working deeply religious people who would bring their twangy language, hillbilly ways, religion and strange music with them. Bluegrass giant Bill Monroe would later popularize their music and become famous throughout the world for his twangy singing style. Other country and bluegrass entertainers growing up in this same area included Martha Carson, Loretta Lynn and her sister Crystal Gayle, Ricky Skaggs and Gary Brewer. Most Kentucky newcomers to Indiana would never lose that twang. You knew they were from Kentucky as soon as they spoke their first word to you but they could never hear this accent themselves. But that twang was as much a part of them as the color of their own eyes.

They were used to "farming" a small patch of corn planted alongside a mountain, utilizing a couple of horses or mules, and tending a lone milk cow. Jokingly enjoying telling others about having to "hang onto the cornstalks" to keep from falling and rolling down off the mountain, they were enthralled with lushly green, fertile, gently rolling Jackson County. And even though they brought their horses and mules with them to these new farms, they would soon learn that animal power was not enough in Southern Indiana's rich loamy soils. They would soon discard the animals in favor of tractors and other modern conveniences.

Two miners with their carbide headlamps on their helmets are riding on a mining locomotive. (Wainscott photo)

The menfolk were also tired of working, often times on their knees, deep within the damp, cold confines of the underground coal mines, always fearful of a cave-in. The air they breathed in contained the powdery silica residue of the coal dust when it was blasted or picked from the rich veins. It damaged their lungs with every breath they took. Many of them suffered terminal lung damage recognized much later legitimately as "Black Lung Disease" from their mining days, but still they were wary of moving away from the region until others had gone before them. Slowly, and then faster and faster, many dared to make the big move away from everything they held dear.

As word drifted back from those who had dared to move away to those still stuck in the hills of the riches of the farmland, the surfeit of jobs to be had, many others started the trek to Indiana and other states. For years the Hoosiers would say that the Kentucky schools taught not just the 3-R's but 4-R's. This included Reading, 'Riting, 'Rithmetic and Route 31 North. My Dad made many trips north in his old 1947 Dodge flatbed truck, each time moving another family and their belongings and livestock to Jackson County. The old Dodge was one of thousands that had been produced for war use but was still sitting in a box unassembled until about a year or so before Dad acquired it. By that time it was assembled and he only needed to construct a bed for it.

My Parents, Kenneth and Rachel Day

Then, our family became one of those migrants.

My Dad, Kenneth Day, worked sometimes miles deep underground in the coal mines for 26 years with much of that time spent in such cramped spaces, he worked on his knees. I had four older brothers who were approaching the age to be able to quit school and go to work in the mines and my parents did not want them to stop their education and start in the mines. So my parents, older brothers, two sisters, a younger brother and I made the move to Jackson County in November 1948. I was six years old at the time.

That decision to move evolved slowly over several months time. Such drastic change had to be discussed and thought about for a long time. Many prayers were offered to the heavens seeking guidance on the issue of moving.

Dad and my Mother, Rachel, operated a small family-oriented grocery store in a tiny community in the foothills of Pine Mountain called Day, named after the many Day residents in the area. The store also included the local post office, which Mother operated.

That store, along with its official contingent of U. S. mailboxes had provided a pretty good living for our family. Every shelf was filled to sagging capacity with canned produce and stalks of bananas hung from hangers anchored in the ceiling. Sacks of feed for all kinds of animals were stacked alongside one of the walls. Barrels of salt fish and pickles stood in front of the long wooden counter. You could literally buy anything that was available at the time in this small grocery. An old wooden bench was placed around the woodstove so the visitors could sit and warm a spell in cold weather or just swap news and yarns in warm weather. The bench was sort of the hub of the store; anything worth telling was told while sitting on or standing near that bench.

During the war years mother sold certain items from the store, accepting her customer's ration tickets that had been issued to them to buy their necessities by the US government. I can remember sitting on the floor of the store while she waited on her customers, playing "store" with my younger brother and sister while the older ones were in school, using the ration coupons as cash. Even as a child I recognized these coupons as cash. Once Mother had a stash of them they would be redeemed and the government would pay her cash for those she sent to them.

Dad owned a large flatbed truck to haul the groceries and feed to the homes of his customers and to operate a rural mail route and taxi service. (See picture on cover of a similar old truck.) His customers would get paid on Friday and that evening or that weekend they would crowd into his store to pay their bills from the week before and order delivery of their grocery necessities and animal feed for the following week. Those days were always busy and hectic for everyone. Dad always offered, and the offer was always accepted, to drive the customers home and help them off-load their purchases.

Train at Tipple having Coal Loaded

Dad actually worked three jobs and mother two to support our family in Kentucky. Mother ran the store and sorted the mail into the postal bins that sat to the side on a portion of the counter. Dad worked nights in the coal mines, returning home before dawn with the lighted carbide lamp on his helmet and the stars overhead providing his only illumination. The smell of burning carbide is in my nostrils even today. He was so black with coal dust all we could see of him would be the pink inside of his lips, his white teeth and the whites of his eyes until after he had taken his bath. After his warm bath he ate a quick breakfast then would get in that truck and drive several miles to the head of Cowan Creek to start his next job.

From there he would pick up any mail from mailboxes along the roadway as he returned; accepting riders in the back of that truck who needed a ride to town or to work. I believe he charged a fee of ten cents each direction for riders. Then he would stop at Mother's post office, pick up any mail Mother had sorted and bagged and continue on to the big town of Whitesburg. Once there he would leave the mail at the postoffice and drop off his riders. He would return home, dropping any mail to Mother that he had collected in Whitesburg that needed sorting then fall, dead to the world, into bed for a few hours of much needed sleep. That evening he would waken, run back into Whitesburg and pick up his riders; returning to our postoffice to pick up the sorted mail for those living up the holler and deliver it and his riders. It was hectic but both of them maintained this kind of pace for many years.

Now the truck was to be put to another use. It would move many families including ours to Southern Indiana.

After several times of his coming to the small community of Kurtz bringing the belongings and members of other related families, he found a farm he liked alongside State Road 58 and decided to buy it. The farm contained 96 very fertile rolling green acres, perfect for running steers and milk cows on. It was even more perfect to raise his eight children on. And, best of all, there was an elementary and high school within three miles and a school bus route went right by the farm. Having a high school close by was very important to Dad and Mother who wanted all of us to get as much education as we possibly could. Without even consulting Mother, Dad put down a down payment and signed a contract to purchase the farm for our family.

Not since the Dust Bowl days of the 1930's when the Okies from Oklahoma migrated to California in search of a better life, chronicled in the book 'The Grapes of Wrath" had there been such a modern day exodus of a group of people from one area of the United States to another. Because so many mountaineers decided to migrate the demographic statistics of several states such as Michigan, Indiana, Kentucky and Ohio would be forever changed.

So, much like Jed Clampitt of television fame who left his beloved Tennessee hills and moved to Beverly Hills, California, our family sold its familiar home and prosperous business then loaded up and moved to Southern Indiana. It would turn out to be the best decision Dad ever made for us.

4 versions of Lynch mine opening over the years.

Goodbye to Cowan Creek

Once the decision had been made to move to Indiana preparations to leave started taking shape immediately. Our move had to be orchestrated with great forethought so that our large family would have what it needed to exist on if Dad took some earlier loads to the North before we actually left ourselves.

Dad decided to sell our milk cow to his brother, Pat, but would take the two horses, Bill and Charlie. The horses would be moved first, along with some hay and other feed. He could place them at the farms of other friends already there until we actually got moved. Only the essentials would be held back for the last trip down the Cowan Creek road.

Dad's family, from left, Anita, Pat, Mama Day, Margie, Dad, Madge and our other Grandmother, Mama Caudill.

Our possessions were sorted out, cried over and discarded or given to others. The decision to leave or take things would sometimes be difficult and very emotional ones.

Dad sold our store to his brother Pat lock , stock and barrel. Pat had been wanting it for some time, envious of Dad's success perhaps. He would find out within six months that it was not an easy job keeping the store stocked with fresh goods and waiting on customers. Uncle Pat had no means of transporting the groceries and feed purchased from him by his customers to their homes and they had no means to do so themselves. Too, after so many residents had left the hills, many of those remaining to serve as his customer base had very little money with which to pay him so they quickly fell behind in their grocery bills. Within six months or so Pat quietly closed the store and the community never had a grocery again. He and his family would follow ours to Indiana. Once here he stayed for a short time, returned to Kentucky for awhile, the returned once again to Indiana for the final time.

But before any move could be made there needed to be a going away party, Mother decided. She and the "hired girl" started making preparations for the party while they sorted our goods. The "hired girl" was not a maid as such, we could not afford one; but Mother had a young woman she occasionally hired to assist her since all of us girls were too young to be of much help to her. Cakes and cookies were baked; homemade fudge, divinity and other candies were cooked and hidden from the eager hands of the children; breads of all descriptions were baked so the night before we were to leave enough food would be available to feed everyone who would be attending our party.

A lot of the treats they prepared ahead of time were placed in buckets attached to ropes which ran over pulleys and the buckets lowered down into the cold water of our dug well in the backyard just off the porch. This was our "refrigerator" for a long time. Homemade butter and fresh milk would be placed in similar, lidded buckets and lowered down into that cold mountain water and it never failed to stay fresh. Dad had rigged a crossbar just under the roof of the well-house, which was walled up from the depths of the well to about three feet above the earth, with stone excavated from the hole. On this crossbar Dad rigged several pulleys with ropes for each pulley. You had to look down into the well to see which rope you needed to pull up to retrieve whatever you wanted to use. The idea was crude, but it worked extremely well. The water coming out of any mountain stream was icy cold.

A big sign was made and placed at the end of our lane announcing our going away party. Soon word was passed from mouth-to-mouth and house-to-house all up and down that end of the mountain that we were leaving and we were inviting everyone to our going away party. Dozens of Mother's women friends and customers made their own plans to attend and started preparing food to bring with them to the party. This was to be a huge occasion, probably the biggest one in the area since the war's end and the people needed a diversion. So many of their friends had already gone from the area they were lonely. Now our family, one they had depended upon the most, was leaving and we would be sorely missed by everyone who had ever done business with us.

Dad was sent far away somewhere to buy a large number of fireworks. They were to be set off at the very end of the party as our final goodbye to all our friends.

On the day the party was to be held the older boys were sent with brooms to the new concrete bridge which spanned the creek in front of our house. The roadway was still gravel and would not be paved for several more years. The state had recently built a new concrete-floored bridge over Cowan Creek right in front of our house. With the gravel on the road, every time a car went up or down the creek, which was rare because there were very few automobiles at that time, the loose gravel would be kicked up on the bridge floor.

Since that bridge would become our dance floor that night the boys were sent there to sweep it clear of any gravel which could have caused someone to fall.

Lighting was strung up on extension cords stretching from the store to a pole set up by the bridge. Electricity had only been placed up and down the creek a few months earlier so this was kind of rare, but we did have it.

Late that evening people began streaming down out of the mountains and roads to the bridge and to the end of our driveway. Kids slipped away from their parents to play in the cold waters of the creek. It was shallow the day of the party but after a rain it could become a raging torrent as it meandered down the holler squeezed in as it was between two steep foothills. While the kids were enjoying themselves the men were hunkered down with their butts resting on one foot, telling tales, and expressing their loss in our leaving to Dad. They could sit for hours in this position without tiring.

The womenfolk were either setting their food baskets on long trestle tables placed in the area for that purpose, keeping an eye on their children or in the kitchen with Mother helping her finish her preparations for the party.

Finally, it was nearly dark, and all us kids were almost starving, a veritable mountain of food was uncovered and everyone fell to with a vengeance. Not a bite would be left uneaten when all was said and done, but Mother had saved some fried chicken and other treats for us to eat on our trip the next day. Even the hound dogs would be well fed and sated on our scraps, falling down on their sides for a little snooze. Then Mother's special treat food, still hidden in the well of course, was brought up and it too was enjoyed.

What a good time everyone had.

After the meal and desserts had been eaten it was quite dark except under where the electric lights shown down. The mountain musicians stepped forth with their fiddles, mandolins, guitars, jugs, and washboards; our Aunt Anita (Dad's youngest sister) stepped up to do the square dance calling; everything was ready for the dancing to begin.

Several "squares" of eight people were formed and the musicians struck up the band. Anita started calling the instructions and the dancers were soon swirling merrily around on that concrete bridge. I don't remember what it's weight load was rated, but I bet that load limit was nearly met that night. The musicians would play reels as fast as they could play, sometimes breaking a string or two. That one would drop out to make repairs but someone else would take their place while new strings were placed on their instruments, then back in the melee they would step. The dancing would go on for hours and hours, until Dad called a halt near midnight by setting off one of the big Roman candle fireworks he had ready and prepared. We needed some sleep before we started to Indiana the next day so his grand finale was the fireworks display and it was spectacular.

I am reproducing Aunt Anita's square dance calls here for your enjoyment with permission from her daughter, Carolyn Sturgill:

Aunt Anita's square dance calls:

Circle left and let's get them straight,
Swing your partner and promenade eight.
Stop at home and watch the lead.

Off to the left in a wild goose chase,
Back to the right in a gander pace.
Red bird's eye and a pigeon's wing,
Everybody let your left hand swing.
Now your own, everybody swing
And promenade home.

Swing the one who stole the sheep,
Now the one who ate the meat.
Now the one who gnawed the bone,
Now the one you call your own.

Aunt Anita

Wind up six in two little bunches,
The old cow kicks and the little calf hunches.
Bow Wow. Shoot that owl.
Swing your honey and she'll follow you
Right over here where you started from.

Around to the back and take a little peek,
Back to the center and swing your sweet.
Around to the back and take another peek,
Back to the center and swing your sweet.
Side couple swing and promenade home.

Right hands cross and how do you do,
Left hand back and shake your shoe.
Eight hands up and hug 'em girls.
Opposite swing. Now your own.
Everybody swing and promenade home.

Box them gnats. Right, Left.
Right over here and cheat this man.
If you can't cheat him, I know who can,
Circle left and let's get them straight.

Lady around gent and gent go slow,
Lady around gent and gent don't go,
Right hand swing.
Wave the ocean, wave the sea,
Wave that pretty girl back to me.

All the way around to #1,
place her back where you got her from.
On around to #2,
Place her back like you ought to do.
On around to #3, put her back,
She belongs to me.
On around to #4,
I'll swing her and take her home.

The Maypole Song and Dance

One and one is two,
two and three are five,
winding up the Maypole
sure as you're alive, sure as you're alive.
Winding up the maypole, sure as you're alive.

This is the last dance and is danced as the caller sings the Maypole song. The couples dance counter-clockwise in a circle, holding hands tightly. The lead dancer releases the hand of the person in the couple next to him. He leads the group through and under that couple's clasped hands. He turns opposite, or right, and circles back around to dance through the next couple and so on. The entire group continues to dance in a counter-clockwise circle. When the lead dances through all of the couples, he then clasps the persons hand he first released, thus completing the circle. The caller says, "Put your sore toes in your pockets." He/She again sings the Maypole song changing the word "up" to "down." The group then dances backwards and clockwise. The lead dancer reverses the dance to unwind. This circle dance is complicated, but lots of fun.

Once the last fireworks was launched and the oohs and aahs of the children had stopped, the mountain women started gathering their sleepy, tired children together for the long walk home. The men shook hands with Dad and the older boys; the women cried as they told Mother goodbye. It was a sad, sad time for all.

After the crowd had gone we went to bed for a few hours of much needed sleep. Early the next morning before daylight broke over the mountain we were rousted from our warm beds; then they were knocked down and placed inside the big flatbed truck. Once the cookstove and all the remaining furniture was loaded and we kids were inside the truck, a heavy tarp was placed over the truck. This was for protection of our goods and warmth for us because it was mid-November and the weather was quite cool.

The older brothers climbed aboard, anxious to get started on the long road northward. Mother sat in the truck's cab with Dad and Anna Ruth, with Major still just a baby on her lap so she could nurse him when needed. The brothers were not too happy to have me back there with them because they all knew how carsick I became when I was a passenger in any vehicle. I never disappointed them.

During the loading of our furniture, the couch was placed in the truck last with it facing to the rear and a couple of chairs, one on each end of the couch for us kids to sit on during the long eight to ten hour truck ride. The tailgate was only half-high and the upper portion was left uncovered so we could sit on the chairs and couch and see behind us. We were then ready to begin and Dad started his truck's engine.

As early as it was when we left our home, as we were driving slowly down Cowan Creek taking one final look, we found the roads were lined with our friends and neighbors. They, too, had gotten up early and ran to the road so they could wave to us one final time. We waved to them and my older brothers leaned out the back over the tailgate, shouting, "You better come with us, we're going to Indiana." Some of my brothers' jeers were not that polite either. Our brothers were anxious to leave, they were ready and would miss their many friends, but could not understand why everyone would not want to move.

We would drive Kentucky highways for several hundred miles and many hours, winding along rivers, between mountains and through tiny towns and bigger cities, with me puking all the way, before we reached Indiana Route 31 North just above Louisville. Dad stopped once somewhere along the way and bought a bottle of beer. He left it with my brothers with instructions to feed it to me a bit at a time so I could clear my stomach. It worked so well doing this trip that I was never able to drink a beer in my life. As soon as a mouthful hits my stomach, my stomach rebels and it comes right back up.

We stopped only a few times along the way north to gas the truck up or to use the bathroom, usually alongside the roadway because that was the only alternative, and once or twice to eat some of the food Mother had prepared the day before.

We would arrive at our destination exhausted, dirty, smelly from my sick stomach and ravenous. But no one could go to bed yet. Mother somehow fixed us a small meal while the men were unloading the beds and setting them up. We would fall into those beds and sleep the sleep of the dead, but on the morrow we were ready to view our new domain.

Once again, we woke to the smell of breakfast cooking in the kitchen with Mother standing in front of that old wood cookstove. Our world was now back in its familiar orbit with Mother in the kitchen and good smells wafting from there. We eagerly headed out after breakfast to examine our new surroundings and become familiar with the new world around us.

Those Left Behind

The migration of so many talented, intelligent people left such a vast hole in the remaining population it would be many years before the area completely recovered. It was a nearly complete "brain drain" on the community when this many dynamic forward-looking people left in such a short period of time. During a two-year period beginning about 1946 through 1948, dozens of these leading families moved away from this depressed area.

But with the declining coal mining industry being the single employer of every able bodied man who wanted to work, those who wanted "better" had to leave to find better. There was no other choice for them to make since the coalmines offered their only opportunity to support their growing families.

Many of those families who left had at one time lived in "coal towns." A coal town was a small settlement owned by the mining companies. The men who toiled in the mines were paid in coal company script instead of money issued by the U. S. Mint. The mine owners actually nearly owned the miners. The mine owners provided miners their housing and a rent assessment was deducted from their pay chits. The remaining chits could be redeemed for food and clothing at the company owned store, thereby making the miner almost a slave. It took a very determined man and woman to escape the chains of this type of slavery. I was born in one of these towns, called Benham. There was another called Blackey, and probably many others besides just these two.

Picture of coal train thru mine town

I don't mean to imply that only the dumb ones remained in the mountains, because that is not entirely true. But there were so few really capable men and women left to lead, that the area would need a long time to heal the rift this mass exodus caused. It would not be until President Lyndon B. Johnson started his "war on poverty" programs in the 1960s that any amounts of money or prosperity would return to this region of Eastern Kentucky.

President Johnson started guaranteeing each family a monthly income to support itself. This very quickly became known as "The Dole." While some viewed this as a shameful thing to be on—much like welfare—no one had the personal resources to be able to turn away from it, so they accepted the government's money. By accepting this government handout they were able to buy foodstuffs for their tables and clothing for their bodies. They were once again able to adequately, but meagerly, feed their children the necessities they needed to survive. Regional medical centers were built to address their coalmining related health issues. Head Start learning and feeding programs would be started in every mountain school to ensure every child received at least one hot meal each day. The wide-eyed sad looking children in this area no longer had to go to bed hungry. The Dole didn't provide for every want, but it certainly helped these people meet their basic needs.

It also hurt many of them. Those that accepted the money and slacked off in their own efforts to support themselves soon became a blot on the mountainside. Some in this group had always raised a garden, a pig and milked their own cow. Now they no longer did even that small amount of work, electing instead to sit on their porches with their feet propped on the porch rail and wait for their monthly Dole. They became extremely lazy and expected the "Guv'ment" to keep them. But the ones who accepted the Dole and continued with their own efforts, were remarkably better off. This group would go forward and produce the next generation's leaders.

Even today if you are traveling through this region you may be stopped in the roadway for a long time as the streets in the larger towns are so crowded you cannot move forward. I asked about this once when I was going "home" to visit and was told that the families had received their "Dole" the day before and they had been doing their shopping.

The people who migrated to Indiana were the healthiest of the lot, the most ambitious, and the better-educated group. Those remaining in the mountains could never see the logic or understand why our families wanted to move away. The remaining mountaineers were content to stay where they had lived their lives so far but they would remain much poorer for their decision to stay.

While the migrants left a gaping hole from whence they had come, especially in the churches and the schools in that area, they filled like places in Indiana with a virtual glut of new idealists.

These new Hoosiers were proud. Those tall, strong, good looking "men" attending the local high school always left home each morning wearing a freshly starched and ironed white shirt with the long sleeves rolled very carefully to just below the elbow, showing their hard, tanned muscular forearms. Because of the hardships they had suffered in the mountains, their decision to move north, and their many different experiences in life, most would have considered this group of males as men rather than boys. They were always careful in their grooming and some of the Indiana "boys" resented their presence, especially around their girlfriends. Some pretty rough fights ensued because of this rivalry. The girls were, of course, very interested in these very handsome new men of the neighborhood and showed it by flirting outrageously with them. These new guys added a wonderful new mix of characteristics to the local gene pool.

Many of the new females in the school were also very beautiful. For the most part they were dark eyed beauties with lovely waving auburn hair and slim figures. They would provide nice viewing for the very boys who were put off by the appearance of their brothers. Many of these girls would marry local boys when the time came for them to marry.

A lot of the men in the families coming from Eastern Kentucky followed in the footsteps of their fathers when selecting a mate. Their wives would be chosen not only for their beauty, but also for their being able to take care of and manage the family hearth; raising their children in the only way they had ever seen children raised.

They mostly married for life and few of the wives of these young men would ever see the need to leave and seek jobs outside their homes. Some could have worked out of their homes if they had wanted to, and a very few did so, but the men actually frowned on the idea. The men earned a good living and they wanted their wives to remain in and maintain their home. It was up to the wives to wise spend and save some of the money earned by the men and rear any offspring they might have in an acceptable manner. I don't recall anyone having a need to call on the welfare lady to help them pay their bills. If they needed to purchase something or owed anyone money, they somehow found the funds to pay their own way.

These new people would give freely of their talents to the communities to which they had moved, in the process, increasing the value of all around them. They could plow and plant a field or garden, build houses, barns and other structures and drive anything on wheels. There was literally nothing they could not learn to do and they were always eager to lend a hand. The businesses in the north loved these men and hired them to be leaders of men.

Uncle Ned

One of the men who remained behind and one who actually profited handsomely from coal mining was our Uncle Ned.

Uncle Ned had always been a character, shunned by some in the family because of his alcoholism, but I always loved him because of his colorful character. He was of average height with a shining bald head, one of only two bald-headed Day men I ever knew. The other was his brother, Uncle Ran, who died not many years after we moved to Indiana.

While it is true Ned had a problem with his alcohol, he was also a very astute business-man and a red hot Republican. He used to come to our house when he had been drinking and pay each one of us children a quarter to say we would be Republicans when we grew up. We accepted the quarters, of course, because that was a vast sum of money to children who never had a penny. Then when he sobered up in a day or two, he would return and ask Mother to make each of us return the money. She refused and we made a lot of quarters in this way.

When Ned was finished with his booze bottles he would place them in the loft area of a small storage house behind his main house. These bottles were quite beautiful and probably would be collector's items today if they were still there. Sadly, after I had married and my husband and I, along with our two boys who were collecting bottles at that time visited Ned, the storage building's loft was bare.

He had reformed years before and gotten rid of his pretty bottles, he told us.

Ned lived to the left of our house if you were standing in the road facing our house. Between us lay the Day family cemetery and Ned's goose pens. Nearly everyone kept geese so they could make pillows and featherbeds and he was no exception. The geese were penned in a small run under the pawpaw tree grove and they alerted Uncle Ned every time a visitor was coming up or down the road.

They always alerted him when I attempted to walk across the full-length log that bridged the creek to his place. I have been afflicted with vertigo my entire life and each time I attempted to walk the log to Ned's place, I would get dizzy, lie down on the log and hang on for dear life. I could look down and see that water moving and would swear it was going upstream at a fast rate. Screaming like a banshee I would have been stuck there on that log to this day except that Uncle Ned would come down the 20 or so stone steps from his house to the creek and pry my frozen fingers from that log and carry me across.

It was great fun to visit his house. It sat on a small knoll, and as I say it had 20 big stone steps up to the front porch. Lining the walkway were bunches of pampas grass which gave the house sort of a ghostly visage as the grasses waved eerily in the wind. But the house was spectacular to a young girl.

It was the only one of its kind in that area that inspired my imagination to think of Gone With the Wind's fantasy plantation, Tara. It was two stories tall and had a wide front porch with about five or six wide wooden steps up onto the porch and had a suspended porch swing on the left end. Once you entered through the front door you were in the living room which had a fireplace on the right end with a black bearskin rug lying on the floor in front of it. The bear's mouth was wide open and it had huge yellow fangs and yellow glass eyes. Along all the walls in that room were stuffed animal heads—elk, moose, deer, bear—from Ned's hunting expeditions.

On a landing half-way to the second story sat a really nice spinning wheel that had been used for ages to spin the cloth for the family's clothing. I loved that thing. I never felt I had been "home" when I was grown until I had visited with Uncle Ned and looked up that stairway to see that spinning wheel.

His mother, my great-grandmother Maude, was very, very old and I remember her as being an invalid with long stringy gray hair. Her hands and fingers were long and bony with long hard fingernails and each time I visited I would be made to visit her in the bedroom and lean over that bed and kiss her on the cheek. She was well over 100 when she died when I was three, but I remember her funeral very well.

At that time all the funerals and wakes were held in the homes of the deceased. Maude was "laid out" in a pretty dress and her casket was open and set upon sawhorses in the living room. The family would sit up with the dead, day and night, until after the funeral which was usually held the very next day because embalming was not a practice at tht time. While the women of the family bathed and dressed the dead, the men would be building a casket and digging a grave. Once the funeral was over, the family would be fed a huge meal, I assume to assuage in some way their loss, then all would walk back to their own homes.

The day of his mother's funeral Uncle Ned was very drunk. He went upstairs, raised the window over the porch and peed down over the roof, causing a real stir among the mourners sitting out on the front porch and saw it dripping off the tin roof. We kids were playing in his yard under the pampas grass clumps and found a discarded condom. Not knowing what it was we had found, we went running inside the house with it hanging from our hand asking all the grownups what it was. One finally grabbed it and disposed of it. All in all it was a memorable day.

To the right away from the porch were several bee hives made from 3 foot pieces of hollow sycamore tree trunks. The hives were surrounded by very mushy ground, probably mole runs, now that I am old enough to know about such things, that Ned told us was haunted ground. I'm sure he told us that to keep us away from the danger of the bees. But for my entire childhood I believed the ground was haunted.

Just up the lawn from the bees in the side yard was a string of about six or seven small shacks, each attached to its neighbor and used mainly for storage at that time. Ned told us these small houses had originally been slave cabins. That part of his tale is probably true since it is a documented fact that our ancestors kept slaves. Many slaves remained on the property after emancipation until their own death and were buried with reverence in their part of the family cemetery.

But Ned was really a brilliant man. He spent his entire life traversing the country, raising funds to build churches of all denominations and for his beloved Republican party. He was the only Presbyterian member of the entire family that I know of. All the remaining members were staunch Old Regular Baptists.

When I decided to throw my hat into the political ring here were I live in 1976, I drove down "home" with Dad and Mother and visited with Ned. He gave me a lot of free advice about politicking, but he had mellowed over the years. It bothered him not a whit that I was running on the Democratic ticket. He said he was glad I had the guts to run for an office. He wrote me several letters that year, building up my confidence, giving political advice, etc. I just wish I had kept them, but alas, I did not.

When coal was discovered on Uncle Ned's property the coal company found that he was the rare one who had not sold his mineral rights to a coal company years before. The mining companies used what they termed "Broad Form Deeds" which essentially stole the minerals from the landowners for an absolute paltry sum of money. The land owners would find they had no recourse in the courts of law and would be at the mercy of the company. Ned not only sold his coal to the mining company for a fee, he charged it a another fee for every ton driven over his property and another fee for every truck moving across his property pocketing a nice bit of change.

Ned, like many in our family who lived long lives, would live to the ripe old age of 88 then commit suicide because he had become confined to a wheelchair and could no longer pursue his interests. I certainly will never forget this remarkable man and how he triumphed over the mining company. The local newspaper honored him in death by starting his obituary on the front page, using half a page of the available space, and continuing inside with another whole page. He will long be remembered.

Mother and the Church

As happy as the new families were with their new farms, jobs and schools, they soon discovered that the area lacked one essential element. There was no Old Regular Baptist church anywhere nearby. The tiny town of Kurtz where many of them lived, population about 125, contained only a Nazarene church and the mountain bred Baptists were very wary of this church. Its tenets were totally unfamiliar to the Baptist's whole way of life and a small friendly competition for the new youths would begin and go on for years between the two congregations.

Picture of the Old Regular Baptist Church

This lack of a church presented a big challenge to the staunch church-going mountain Baptist people. Dad and Mother would meet with his devout distant cousins, Ivory and Loren Day who lived nearby with their families, to discuss the issue.

They were not such fundamentalists that they believed in snake handling, but their view of religion was very austere. All of the new residents were aware of snake handling practices back in the mountains and elsewhere in the South, but this group shunned such matters. It was never a part of their religious practices.

I remember one time when I was about five years old and my sister Sylvia and our cousin Jessie Fern, both about 7, sneaked under the tent flap of a snake handling tent revival to see what was going on. We were very curious but this was strictly against the direct order of Jessie Fern's mother, our aunt Evie. Evie was Mother's brother Watson's wife and they had only the one girl. Sylvia and I often visited them in Cumberland for several days at a time.

Anyway, Evie knew the tent revival was going on and knew we would be curious but strictly forbade us to go anywhere near the "Holy Rollers" as she referred to them. The Holy Rollers were not Baptists, but maybe they were Pentecostal members, which is similar in many ways to both religions. Aunt Evie let us out of the house to play and made us promise we would not go near this tent.

You can guess what happened after that. We three could not resist just going over there and taking a quick peek. I guess when we ran home, nearly hysterical after watching those people handle those rattlers and letting them twine around their arms, Aunt Evie figured out what we had been up to.

Our aunts and uncles were never ones to wait for someone else to do it, so Evie cut herself a limber switch and used it on all three of us. She certainly didn't need permission from our parents. When we were at her house she assumed the parent role and dealt the punishment out accordingly. All of this discipline was before the days when the parents were not allowed corporal punishment of children without fear of being arrested and jailed.

But now I want to get back to the lack of a church in Indiana. While visiting Dad's cousins' homes in Indiana, Mother and Dad and the cousins would sing and pray but without a minister or someplace to meet formally they were nearly bereft.

This situation went on for several months. Then like a bolt from the blue Mother came up with an idea.

As Mother sat before the large commercial ironing machine that Dad had bought to make ironing our clothes easier for her, she absently stared out the living room window at a vacant garage across the street. It had been empty for a long time; in fact it had not been used in years and it stood there like a sentinel waiting for Mother to make the connection in her brain.

The longer she gazed at the building the more convinced Mother became that the Lord was speaking to her and leading her to a solution to the church problem.

When Dad came in from work that night she told him her idea of turning that garage into a church. Dad thought about her idea while he ate his supper and decided he was delighted with the idea and so after supper he and mother visited his cousins and presented the idea to them. They too were overjoyed with the thought of having their own church close by, and plans were immediately put forward to acquire the building.

I don't know how much if anything was paid for the building and surrounding lots, but it had to have been very inexpensive or maybe even free. None of the families had much money at that time. In the back of my mind I am thinking that the couple who lived diagonally across the highway from us owned this building and donated it to the church. If I am wrong about that fact I'm sure the men would have just taken up a collection amongst themselves and paid cash for the building. The decision was made to have Bertha Day, Ivory's wife, write a letter to the church association back in the mountains and ask it to bless the idea and provide a minister.

Either free or bought, the building was acquired and work began immediately converting the old ugly oil spattered garage into a church. Oil was scrubbed from the concrete floor, and the walls were washed down and painted white. Electric lighting was added and a chimney was built so a heating system could be installed.

A large opening for cars to enter on the East side of the building was sealed and new windows were put in that space. A stage area was built in the front of the building and became the pulpit, which also held two pews on each side for the "Sisters and Brothers". Only members could sit in this area on the stage. The areas were segregated with the Brothers on the left side and the Sisters on the right side.

Mother had wanted to have a bell to ring but several years would go by before she located one. She had always been sort of envious of the Nazarene's large belfry with its beautiful sounding bell and wanted one just like it for the Baptist church. The other members were not as exuberant about this addition so the bell sat outside on the ground for many years until it was stolen by thieves, never ringing a single time to announce a Baptist church service.

A table to hold a community water bucket with a dipper inside it was placed in front of the dais; no one worried about catching germs so all would drink from the same dipper. Any left over water in the dipper would be dumped into a second bucket containing ashes on the floor. At first a wood stove, then later a fuel oil stove was installed for heat. Hours before services were due to start the stove would be lit so the room could be at least partially warm by service time.

Once the service started little artificial heat was needed because the preacher kept his flock warmed up.

The itinerant preacher would be at the Kurtz Old Regular Baptist Church on the second Saturday night and Sunday of each month. When that first service was held in the newly renovated building, the church still lacked a certain something. So much had been accomplished for so little money but with so much labor; however, one problem remained. The building echoed and this echo made it difficult to understand and hear the preacher.

Mother also solved that problem. She made a personal visit to a carpet supplier in Brownstown, it may have been Lucas and Ackerman, but I have long forgotten. The owner turned down her request to supply enough free carpet to cover the stage area.

Never one to doubt or lack in faith, Mother urged him to come to a different decision, applying a little shrewd female logic to her argument. "There are a lot of new families moving here and many of them will need linoleum or carpet," she cajoled. "If we tell them how you gave carpet freely to the church, they will buy their own carpet and linoleum from you."

Not long after Mother returned home the store owner came by to ask her how many yards of carpeting she would be needing and what color she would like to have. Mother chose red commercial carpeting for the stage area and before the next church time the carpet was in place and it solved the echo problem. The carpet store owner also threw in a good quality rubber runner to run from the front door all the way to the stage area for good measure. I guess he didn't want to take any chances of offending Mother or the Lord. I'm also sure he was repaid many times over for that generous donation after Mother spread the word of his generosity to the church to all the other members.

The church's association found a preacher living in Charlestown who agreed to come up and preach and let the members decide if they found him acceptable.

Preacher, Brother Dewey and Ila Sexton.

The preacher was a small man with tiny size six feet, but he could make the rafters ring and the congregation sing when he got wound up. Brother Dewey Sexton and his wife, Ila, became the first to lead this eager congregation and they would serve it for many years to come.

There was never a person who could fall asleep during Brother Dewey's preaching. He was an exciting speaker and seemed to nearly float across the pulpit as he preached, one fist pounding into the open palm of the other hand and his tiny patent leather clad feet nearly tapping a tune on the floor. And as was the Baptist custom, he occasionally hollered loudly as he got his breath to extol another point in his sermon. He held a freshly starched and ironed white handkerchief in one hand to wipe the moisture from his face; he would work up a tremendous sweat while preaching. Before he was done he walked the aisles, shaking hands with every person in the house. This hand shaking would be done by every preacher on the stage before the day's preaching was over.

This was a fundamentalist Baptist church and they did not pay their preacher. The only time a collection was taken from its members was when one was sick, injured or burned out. One member or another quietly paid all other expenses.

The preachers did not as a rule attend a seminary either. They preached from their bibles and what they felt in their hearts. They knew scripture as well as those who had had many years of education.

The former Kentuckians found Brother Dewey very acceptable as a preacher and moved their church memberships from Eastern Kentucky to the new church and watched it grow by leaps and bounds.

The members believed in long hair for the women, foot washing and sacrament once each year, and no music in the church. Their voices would provide the music, they believed.

They embraced the "lining" method of singing where a song leader would read off one line of the song. Once that line was almost sung, the next line was quickly lined aloud by the song leader, and it continued until the end. And all songs were sung a cappella.

Television evangelist Greg Dixon from Indianapolis heard about the church and came down several times and taped the services for later special programming.

At the end of every sermon an invitation would be issued for those wishing to be saved to come to the front of the church and admit their sins. Once they had done that and church had ended for the day, they would be taken to the waters of nearby Salt Creek and baptized. The Baptists believed in total immersion and it made no difference to them if the creek was frozen over or not. If someone needed to be baptized, a hole would be chopped in the ice if necessary and down they would go. They always bragged that no one ever took a cold from being baptized.

Mother had made some very loose white dresses for the women to wear during baptism and she kept white silk handkerchiefs to tie into a tignon around their hair. She would pin the dresses at the hem at the bottom between their legs for modesty's sake before their immersion. Once the newly saved arrived and was pinned and ready, two preachers would take control, one holding each arm and lead the saved into the water. They would each place a hand behind the person to give support; the saved would hold their nose with one hand, and down they went. Much singing and praying accompanied these actions and if several were due to be baptized, this could go on a long time.

On church Sundays there would sometimes be two to six or more preachers up on stage and all would be given a turn to preach. Most of them accepted this offer. Often it was well after noon before they tired and the members were dismissed to eat their dinners.

On Sundays other than their own church time, the members might drive to another community and attend another Old Regular Baptist Church since by the mid 1950's they were beginning to crop up all over Southern Indiana.

Eating and sleeping presented a problem on church weekends in the early days. As difficult as it is now to believe, at that time in the early 1950's there were no restaurants anywhere nearby and no motels at all. Those traveling a long distance to attend church stayed in the homes of the local members and ate with them before leaving for home.

Our house was always a favorite of Brother Dewey and his wife. He loved Mother's soft, sweet-smelling beds and her cooking. They always stayed with us and we looked forward to their visits. Brother Dewey was an easygoing man away from the church and a lot of fun and we kids enjoyed teasing him a good deal. He always wore a suit and a long silk tie, and with his shiny leather shoes looked to be a real dandy. Ila, his wife, was very prim and proper and her stout frame was always well corseted. She always wore a little pillbox hat, hose, heels, and a fancy dress. Her slightly blue gray hair was "done" regularly at a beauty salon in Charlestown and although she was a very nice lady she was much harder to tease.

Finally, after many years, the Baptist congregation had outgrown its building, which was good. A search was begun for another location.

James Aaron & Edith Hampton Ison,.

A faithful friend of the church, James Aaron Ison and his wife, Edith Hampton Ison, told the members they would donate a portion of their farm south of Freetown on which a new church could be built. Their offer was gratefully accepted and drawings were prepared.

Members began the work of erecting the new building. They provided the labor and shopped frugally for the materials until the church was finally finished and they moved into it. When it was finished they didn't owe a penny on it. The sanctuary was much larger than their old one had been; and it had very high ceilings and tall windows. A wide double door stood at the entrance. Off to the right side of the entrance bathrooms were added, a real innovation from the old church's outside privies. A basement had been built under the main sanctuary to provide room for a fellowship hall. You could enter the basement through a door and down some stairs on the left side of the entry doors, or via a sloped handicapped entrance on the right outside of the building. A nice tall spire was added to the front above the entrance, but still no sign of a church bell was seen. A small cross topped the spire instead.

Now the Valley Home Old Regular Baptist Church can be found by turning east off State Road 135 south of Freetown in Jackson County onto county road 540 North, then turning left about a mile up the road onto county road 425 West. The church is about a 100 yards up 425 on the left side.

As the congregation started aging and members started dying off a new problem became apparent. A place was needed to bury their dead without having to take the bodies all the way back "home" to Kentucky. Many wanted to be buried here near their new homes, but they didn't want to lie in a graveyard with "strangers," read that to say Nazarenes.

Again, the Isons donated land. Next door to the church and surrounded by beautiful hardwood trees was a small plot of land that would be ideal. It was on a small shaded knoll, well drained and easily accessible and was ideal for the purpose it was intended.

The cemetery was laid out and plots number and assigned. Now the Old Regular Baptist dead would never have to lie beside strangers. They now had their own cemetery and they were happy. Ivory Day, one of the charter members of this congregation would occupy the first grave in this cemetery.

Picture of the cemetery

The cemetery is kept in pristine condition with regular mowing and trimming and a headstone must grace every grave. That is a rule my Dad insisted on and is another example of their ethics. The mountaineers tended their families in death as well as they did in life.

Eugene Day, the son of Loren Day, one of the original founders of the church, is currently the preacher. Eugene and other ministers have now preached the funerals of many good old Kentuckians with names like Day, Caudill, Ison, Hampton, Sumpter, Frazier, Whitaker, Gilly and Boggs. Those deceased Kentuckians now sleep beneath the sod, their faith in the Lord complete.

Present minister,
Eugene Day and his wife Nezlene

The Two-Room School

The clan I belonged to started its educational endeavors in a very small two-room school known simply as Big Cowan School in the mountains of Eastern Kentucky. We would attend that school until I was six years old and was well into my second grade of school. The two younger children had not yet begun their studies when we moved to Southern Indiana in November 1948.

There were no school buses to take us to our elementary school in Kentucky. We walked to school; therefore there was a very small school every few miles so no one had to walk very far. When the students graduated the eighth grade, they were bused in an old dilapidated school bus to a centrally located high school in a larger town called Whitesburg.

The grade school was small, containing just two classrooms, which had a short hallway near the front entrance that connected the two rooms and gave us a place to store our lunch buckets and coats. The students would place their lunches, usually contained in a clean lard bucket or miner's two-compartment round lunch bucket on a shelf to be eaten at lunchtime and hung their coats on nails. Grades one through four were in one room and grades five through eight were in the other.

Round Miner's lunchbucket

Our lunches usually consisted of cornbread crumbled into milk. One pail would be shared by every child in that family so only one lunch had to be prepared. Sometimes we got peanut butter and jelly or salt pork sandwiches on cold biscuits left over from breakfast. Since the miner's lunch buckets had two compartments we sometimes got cornbread in the top part and soup beans or green beans in the bottom half. They might not have been balanced lunches, but they were filling at least.

There was a blackboard on the wall at the front of each room where the teacher could write our assignments and test work. The teacher's desk sat at an angle near the windows at the front corner so he or she could keep an eye on all the kids at one time. If one misbehaved, punishment was immediate. There was no delay or appeals process. A switch or paddle was in plain sight on the teacher's desk and was frequently used.

A recitation bench was placed in front of the blackboard. When it was a particular class's turn to recite, those students would go there and sit. The other classes would be given assignments to be completed at their desks when not reciting. You could learn a lot by listening to the upperclassmen reciting their lessons aloud. My sister, Sylvia paid particular attention in class and was advanced an extra class but would be placed backward one class in Indiana. I was enrolled when I was barely five years of age. The recitation bench was made by placing a planed split log (to avoid splinters I guess) on short pieces of logs for legs, which were cut from the same tree.

My second grade picture

Our school desks were made in several sizes. Some accommodated one student and others were made to be utilized by two or three students at the same time, depending upon their size I would guess.

Both rooms of the school contained a huge wood- or coal-burning stove. I think coal was most commonly used because it was so readily available and gave off so much heat. This stove sat in the center of each room. If you sat very near it you roasted, if far away, you froze. Only one wall in each room contained windows. They were huge and had many panes of glass and could be opened or closed depending upon the weather. There were no screens on the windows and no fans or air conditioning was available. Electricity had just become reality in that area in about 1946 or so.

Our school's water supply was kind of haphazard. One or two of the students would take a fairly large galvanized bucket to a nearby spring, fill it to the brim with cold fresh water and lug it back to the school where it was poured into large earthenware crocks to keep it cold. Each child had its own glass or tin cup. A dipper was placed in the crock. You would use the dipper to get water from the crock to pour into your cup. No cups were marked, but every child knew which was his.

This method worked well for many years. There were a lot of icy cold springs spewing forth from the mountains. Years after we had moved away a well would be drilled in the schoolyard to make this chore less hard on the students and provide purer drinking water.

Restrooms were located outside the school alongside the creek which flowed nearby and provided the older boys plenty of excuses to get wet. The outhouses were smelly and cold in winter and their only amenity was a Sears Roebuck catalog. Those for both boys and girls were joined by a common wall and were painted white. Each side had a half-moon or sun cut in the door which closed with a bang when a strong spring retracted after the door had been opened. There was no provision made for hand washing after using the bathroom unless one wanted to run to the creek and quickly slosh your hands in the running water.

Many years later a basement was dug under the school in which a cafeteria was installed so the children could have hot lunches. I believe that was done in the 1960's as part of the president's war on poverty program. And the Lord knows this was a desperately poor, poverty-stricken area at the time. For some students these meals eaten in the basement would be their only hot meals of the day; the milk the only portion they would receive.

There was no formal playground as such nor any equipment with which to play. Sometimes there might be some swings the fathers had made hung by ropes from stout tree limbs but they never seemed to last very long. Teachers sometimes provided a jump rope and helped turn it for the younger students, teaching them to recite poems that would help them keep in step as they jumped. I wish I could remember more of those poems today, because they were kind of fun and quite catchy.

The only tune I can remember jumping to goes something like this, "I see London, I see France, I see (supply a name) underpants." If you successfully jumped to this tune, then you would skip out and another child would enter the jump.

The school burned down not long after it went out of use and it and all the tiny schools strewn across the mountains were consolidated into larger schools and students were bussed to the new locations.

The school site was not abandoned. It was kept as a gift to the residents of the area and a beautiful enclosed double shelterhouse was built for family reunions and other events on the grounds. Our huge clan had its first big reunion there because it had a nice dance floor and could accommodate the whole lot of us along with the mountain musicians we had hired.

We moved to Southern Indiana, in Jackson County, in 1948. We were amazed at the progress moving would make. There was a school bus that stopped at our house each morning and night. It would take us to our school located three miles away. But it wasn't a direct route. Our house was located on the beginning of the bus route and every night and morning we got to go up and down many side roads and back roads before the bus was fully loaded and then driven to the school or unloaded in the afternoon.

It was fun. You could pick your own place to sit in the bus as long as you didn't cause a ruckus. In that case you would be assigned a seat, usually just behind the driver, where he could keep a sharp eye on your behavior.

Our new school was huge when compared to our mountain school. It contained over 400 students in grades one through 12. Many of the families had four to eight children, almost all of school age. This created a real problem in some areas as the available classrooms suddenly had to be stretched to accommodate the Kentucky children. With the sudden influx of so many Kentucky pupils a separate school had to be built across the road from the big school to house the kindergarten through six grades, leaving the bigger building for those in grades seven through 12.

Although I had always loved school I now found I really hated it because of my second and fifth grade Indiana teachers. In Kentucky I had been considered a beautiful and very bright child. Attending school nearly every day when I was four years old, they finally accepted me as a student when I was five. I was ecstatic. Now I could go to school and have books of my own. One teacher looked at my first grade picture and said I might grow up to be a movie star. In Indiana some of the teachers were very cruel. My second grade teacher hated Kentuckians with a passion and me in particular it seemed. Her classes were beginning to fill up with several of those twangy-talking Kentuckians and she didn't really like any of us. The fifth grade teacher spent most of each day holding mock weddings, funerals, court etc. or hypnotizing some of the students. I don't think we learned anything from our first male teacher.

In the second grade I got a spanking nearly every day, sometimes more than one. I seemed to cry constantly but was afraid to go home and tell my parents because they told all of us if we got a spanking at school we would get another at home. I have never agreed with parents telling their children this. In my case, it meant this particular teacher was never called to task for her own misdemeanors.

I was born with very poor eyesight and no one realized it until I was ten years old. That seems amazing to me now when every school requires a physical and eye exam every year, but back then that was not the case. You could have had only one eye and no one would have noticed.

Anyway, because of the vision problem I could never see the blackboard from where the second grade teacher assigned me to sit and I would have to ask someone else to read it aloud to me, for which I got whipped regularly. She would not allow me to sit on the front seat for ease in viewing the board. If another child borrowed or loaned me paste or a crayon I got whipped. If the kids were singing a song I didn't know and she noticed I wasn't singing, I got whipped. She even whipped me because I could not see well enough to find an Easter egg during our egg hunt. I not only got a whipping for not finding any eggs, I got another because my best friend gave me three of hers. This teacher would tell the other kids not to play with me because I was one of those "dumb Kentuckians," or say I was "retarded" because I could not see to catch a ball. She would look through my hair in front of the other kids during recess to see if I had lice. She was absolutely sadistic.

I made it a point to tell my own children to come to me and let me know if they had a problem with any teacher in their schools. I wanted to prevent a recurrence of the problems I had. This teacher is now dead and I cannot say I regret her passing and that is shameful, but that is just the way I feel.

The fifth grade teacher was finally dismissed because he dated and married a high school student.

During the summer between my fifth and sixth grades I became very ill and the family doctor could find no physical reason for my pain. I had such a headache I could only prop myself in a corner of the room and cry it hurt so bad. The doctor finally sent me to an optometrist to have my eyes checked and the problem was found and solved. The optometrist found I was legally blind and probably had been since birth and I got my first pair of glasses. My sixth grade teacher realized I had potential and kept me in at recesses and noon hours to tutor me so I could catch up with my classmates. I caught up and passed all but one of them. When I graduated from high school I was second in my class and had been on the high honor roll from the sixth grade on. I have always been grateful to this wonderful man for what he did for me, allowing me to catch up to the other students and

First pix of Helen in Glasses

for realizing I was not stupid or retarded as I had been led to believe.

My classmates were far kinder to me than these two teachers. A few called me four-eyes but not for long. We all became very good friends. That friendship among the entire class of 16 students would last a lifetime as we keep in touch with each other and share our losses and our gains.

Not too many years after I graduated, that high school was closed and consolidated with a much larger school about 20 miles away. I still feel that we learned more in the much smaller schools of days gone by.

It seems when you get several thousand students together in one building, as we do today, you have more discipline problems. It may be true that by consolidating the school systems taxpayers can provide more services and classes, but those small township schools could not be beat.

The Kitchen Table

When one thinks of a kitchen table several things come to mind. The kitchen/dining room is a utilitarian table where food is served to the family. But in our house when I was growing up, the kitchen table served many other of our needs as well.

For instance, back in the good old days, with ten people in the house every inch of space had to be utilized to its fullest and some rooms and furnishings served more than one purpose.

The first kitchen table I can remember in our family kitchen was one that was built by my dad when it became apparent he and mother had started a big family. It consisted of four or five pine boards nailed to a trestle-like affair. There was a chair at either end for each of our parents and two benches, one along either side of the table, for the children.

It sat in the center of the kitchen in front of and just about at the end of the big old wood-burning kitchen cook stove. That stove was huge and black with an oven and a water reservoir on the table end of it and a roomy warming oven above it against the stovepipe.

The table being longer than it was wide, made it kind of handy for the children's shorter arms and reaching hands to serve themselves. We got the food the first time around as it was passed from left to right starting at Dad's plate. From then on if we wanted seconds or thirds, we just reached to retrieve anything else we wanted to eat.

With that many reaching hands or stabbing forks mealtimes could become quite hazardous.

Another table would be purchased after the family started to decrease, but it is this long plank table that holds my attention now.

I can remember huge breakfasts eaten at that table. Mother prepared a vast assortment of foods each and every morning. No one was allowed to leave the house for work, school or play without first eating breakfast. Every child was there every evening to eat supper, not dinner, because dinner was the meal served at noon.

Mother always served a fried, baked or boiled cured meat such as bacon, ham or sausage and even sometimes freshly killed chickens. She mixed and kneaded flour and other ingredients in a dishpan she reserved for mixing biscuit dough and baked about 30 beautiful mouth-watering biscuits each morning. She also made gravy, fried apples and eggs. She set out jams, jellies, freshly churned butter and ice cold milk she had milked and cooled from the previous night's milking. There were also corn flakes for our youngest brother, Major. Sometimes fresh fruits or berries or peaches would be served depending upon the season. For a real treat she would occasionally make us "chocolate gravy", but there is no one who remembers how this was made. It may even have been merely a warm chocolate pudding, but Mother referred to it as chocolate gravy.

If you have never tasted some of these foods you have missed out on a good portion of delicious in your lifetime. Fried apples for example. They were made by peeling, coring and slicing tart apples. Sometimes Mother left the peelings on but I preferred it when she peeled them. She would place a large black cast iron skillet on the wood cookstove, add a big dollop of butter and place the apples on top of that. Add a small amount of sugar and about a half cup of water and cover. Steam until the apples are fork tender and serve along with hot biscuits. You better keep a good sharp eye on them though while they are cooking because they burn very easily.

The local Shoney's Restaurant couldn't hold a candle to what Mother prepared every day. She rose at 4:30 a.m. every day of the week. Dad had to be at work by 6 and sometimes he had to drive 20-40 miles to the job site. Then the others who worked and the ones who were still in school had to eat. Mother always ate her morning meal with Dad. Absolutely nothing on the table except the cornflakes came pre-packaged from a store; Mother prepared it all from scratch every morning from resources she herself had helped produce.

With all this farm-fresh food on our daily table none of us were fat as kids. We worked off the excess calories on the farm doing our chores and playing outside. There was no television to distract us or store-bought toys to play with. If we wanted a toy, we made it with whatever was at hand. There were always chores to be done so we burned prodigious amounts of calories every day.

Supper would sometimes be a repetition of the morning meal as far as quantity is considered, but several vegetables would be added instead of eggs. Instead of biscuits we would enjoy hot crunchy cornbread topped with sweet creamery butter. There is only one way to make a decent pan (or pone) of cornbread and that means it has to be baked in a black iron skillet in a very hot oven until it is golden brown.

I still make my cornbread in my own iron skillet but it is not as big a skillet as the one Mother used. For good cornbread you should preheat your oven to 450 degrees. Place the iron skillet in which you have placed a tablespoon of lard or oil in the oven and preheat the skillet too. For an eight inch skillet I mix up ¾ cup all purpose flour and ¾ cups corn meal; 1 heaping teaspoon baking powder; ½ teaspoon salt; 1 tablespoon sugar. Mix dry ingredients well. Add one whole egg and enough sweet milk to make a barely soupy batter. When the oven's timer dings telling you the oven is hot, pour the excess oil into the batter and mix it in too. Pour the batter into the hot skillet and bake until the top is golden brown, about 15-20 minutes. The bottom should be crunchy when the pone is inverted onto a plate.

At that long pine handmade kitchen table we ate sumptuous meals prepared by loving and busy hands. Often times we kids would sit around that table waiting for the food, smelling the aromas of roasting and baking, nearly drooling we were so hungry. But not a single bite would be eaten until all ten of us sat around that table.

Mother fed not only her family but usually several other visitors too on a nearly daily basis. One of our daily visitors was a very elderly lady who lived just across the street from us next door to the church. Miz Smith, as we called her, visited nearly every mealtime with a squat, (remember them?) one-pound coffee can in which she was going to return to her house filled with "water."

She told Mother one time that someone had drowned a cat in her hand-dug well years before and she didn't want to drink her water, hence her visits to our house.

Let me tell you that can never left our house filled with water. It was always filled with food from our table. One or the other of us kids would later take her a bucket of our well water and pour it in her own water bucket. By doing this Mother made sure that Miz Smith ate properly and she did not have to beg.

When we had company the men were served first, then the women, and finally the children. The only children who ate with the adult women were the infants who had to be fed by the mother. All the others waited. The waiting was sometimes hard when we had been playing, working up our enormous appetites. Seems like we were always hungry, but we were always well fed. When it was just the family eating and no visitors were there, we all ate together at the same time.

I did get kind of tired of eating the bony pieces of chicken though when we had company. I would have loved to have had the opportunity to eat the white meat of a nice, plump chicken breast just once when I was a kid, but that never happened. If I was really lucky, I got a drumstick or the lower back piece and to this day I hate those pieces of chicken. Since the men got first choice, then the women, there wasn't much to choose from when it came time for the kids to eat.

After meals were served, eaten and the table cleared, the table was then used to play board or card games on between Dad and one of the kids (usually me and he always lost), 500 rummy games between Mother and Dad (which Mother always won) or homework. There was always something going on around that table. That big old warm cook stove would be kept burning while we played so it was always warm as toast in the kitchen around that big narrow table.

All of us kids should be real estate moguls today we played so many Monopoly games around that table. I was always appointed or I would volunteer for the job of banker because I was good with numbers. I mostly won every Monopoly game, and I also won the title of cheater, which I would carry for the rest of my life. But I never cheated once though that I can remember, but all my sisters and brothers tell everyone who will listen how I always cheated them when I was the banker. I still say it was just because I was good at numbers and they weren't fast enough to realize that.

After I married I would use the poker playing skills I learned playing against my Dad using match sticks for money to support my own family for six months playing nickel and dime poker before the

Air Force men I worked with caught on to the fact that yes, I could play poker pretty well. I had used Mother's old ploy of pretending I didn't understand things and whipped the socks off every one I played against.

I also remember one time when that kitchen table became an operating table. Our older brothers were chopping wood one day out in the barn lot when the ax head came loose from the handle and the sharp blade struck my brother Glenn in the forehead leaving a gaping gash through the eyebrow and eyelid.

Glenn Day.

The eye itself was not damaged. Glenn was placed on that table, held down and stitches were placed by Mother using plain old Coats and Clark thread which she had laid in a pan of boiling Lysol treated water. Mother's usual disinfectant was warm soapy water with liquid Lysol in it. Then the wound was bound with torn strips of a sheet and several days later, the stitches were removed. Glenn was nearly good as new but would always carry a scar, which seemed to give him a somewhat rakish look. There was no need to pay a doctor's fee when Mother was handy. In our family, as in many in those tight money years, you had to have a life-threatening problem before a doctor was called.

It was only after her "baby", our youngest brother Major, was injured that Mother gave in and started taking us to the doctor in emergencies. She just could not cope with her youngest in splints or when she saw him bleeding, but she sure worked on the rest of us regularly.

That kitchen table served as a learning place for all of us. We did our homework there and we heard the latest news there as mother always read any family letters aloud so we could all enjoy them. Three of our brothers served in the Army during the Korean War, so news from them was shared around that table. Dad's sisters and his mother, our Mama Day, wrote wonderful letters and those were read aloud. "Mail Call" was one of our favorite times of the day as we heard what everyone was up to.

We were lectured there after the meals were consumed on how we could do better and become better people. Our school report cards were opened and evaluated and signed at that table and no matter how well you had done you were always told to do better next time.

After the older boys left for the armed services, our kitchen was remodeled and made smaller. We then had to get a "modern" table. Ours had a gray laminated top of some sort with chrome legs and six chairs. That set would serve for many years then lose its pride of place to a hard rock maple set.

Today the experts say when raising children you should spend one or two evenings per week at the dining table, sharing food, experiences and views with your children. In our house we spent seven evenings per week around that big table. I don't know about you but we got hungry seven days a week, not just two.

My memories of family time spent round that table sharing activities with our parents or with each other are still as bright as ever.

Even though it took me many years to learn how to cook a decent meal for my own family, I hope our two sons feel our old red kitchen table holds special memories for them. I know I spent hours in the kitchen trying to prepare a passable meal that we ate together seven nights out of seven when they were growing up. Sometimes the meals were passable and sometimes not, but we ate them anyway. I never claimed to be Miss Susie Homemaker or Betty Crocker. What do kids do today for the other five nights per week? It makes you wonder, doesn't it.

Roy's graduation picture

Six of us were together after Dad's funeral. From left, Palmer, Anna Ruth, me (Helen), Major, Sylvia and Jim. Not present was Roy and Glenn.

The whole gang of us at Anna Ruth's after Dad's funeral.

The Easter Parade

Easter was a time for us to put on our finery and go to church. It was a time to dye dozens of boiled eggs to be hidden and found by the youngsters on Easter Sunday and to buy chocolate bunnies and other Easter candies.

That is what would have happened not too many years ago. Easter and Christmas were the two times of the year when every woman and child, and most men, would enter church to show off their fine feathers.

To see to the front of the church you had to look forward over a sea of extraordinary hats of every color and description.

The search for the perfect Easter bonnet started many weeks before the actual event. You first had to buy your Easter dress so you would know what kind of hat you wanted to go along with it. Dozens of hats would be tried on before the Murphy's Five and Dime store's mirrors and discarded before the perfect one for your new outfit was selected.

Finally one would be chosen and the store's salesclerk would place your new chapeaux into a beautiful cardboard hatbox and tie it up with a pretty ribbon. The hatbox was as useful and pretty as the hat itself. Often the hatboxes lasted many years after the hat had been forgotten and served as a repository for many treasured items.

Every store continuously played the Irving Berlin song, "Put on Your Easter Bonnet." Or maybe the title was "Easter Parade." I think this song was played to keep you in the mood to shop.

Once the hat was chosen, you would have to have new gloves, white shoes and a new handbag to complete the outfit. (You could never wear white shoes until after Easter back then and you should never wear that color after Labor Day.) All your children would need new clothes and maybe a new pair of dress shoes. All this could take weeks of Saturday shopping and was looked forward to by almost everyone. The Easter outfit ranked right up there with the Christmas play and Santa treats.

I say Saturdays because the stores were not open on Sunday as they are now. Sundays were reserved for church services, large family dinners and lazy afternoons reading the Indianapolis Star newspaper and reading the comics to the younger kids.

But those bonnets were always spectacular. Many had fruit, birds, brims, bows or veils in elaborate arrangements. Others were just shaped colored straw hats with little loops on each side so you could put a hatpin in each side to hold them on. And a lot of the children's Easter hats had a single ribbon around the head just above the 2 or 3 inch brim allowing the ribbon to fall down the little girl's back. If I remember correctly these were called sailor hats and they came in all colors to match any little girl's dress.

I remember my Easter hat of 1959 very well. It not only served me as an Easter hat, but when we met the train at Seymour to go on our senior trip to Washington, D. C. we had to wear a hat, suit, gloves and high heels. Oh, how times have changed! While in Washington we had to wear the hats when we went into fine restaurants to dine.

Now when we want to take a trip we wear a sweat suit for comfort and a pair of tennis shoes and athletic socks. If we wear a hat at all, it is usually a billed cap to keep our hair in place or the sun out of our eyes.

Gone are the days of the glamorous detailed hats of yesteryear. Only the bravest woman will don a hat these days. A fun social group has to be the Red Hat Society for women whose dresses are purple and their hats red. I wish I knew some of them because I used to love to wear pretty hats.

I do remember when my two sons were very small I worked with an older lady who lived with her twin sister. Neither had ever married or had children so they kind of adopted my two on the holidays.

For Easter when the boys were one and three the twin sisters went to a very exclusive children's shop and bought them several matching Buster Brown outfits with shoes and socks to match. I took the boys to Easter church services and it scared them to death when I sent them away to the infant's class and they both wet their pants, ruining the looks of their new Easter outfits. Those Buster Brown outfits would become their favorite clothing.

One Easter I remember my sister Anna Ruth bringing her four kids (later she had another) to Mother's house so the kids could hunt Easter eggs.

Her baby at the time, Jodi, was dressed in a pale pink handkerchief linen dress with a big collar, a wide-brimmed bonnet, ruffled panties, white Mary Jane shoes and lace-trimmed socks and gloves. She carried a tiny little white plastic purse. She was so proud of her outfit. She carried that purse and pranced around all day in her pretty dress. She was about 18 months old at the time and was so cute in her finery. That was probably the last time she wore a dress.

At our Easter egg hunts the grownups would hide the eggs the first time. There would be dozens of them and we tried to hide them so all ages could find them. Anna had five kids, I had two, my brother

Jim had three and my brother Glenn one. That made for a pretty good egg hunt. Sister Sylvia lived in Michigan and didn't get to join in the fun very often. Sometimes other children would join us.

After all the eggs were found the first time, one or two of the older ones would send the little ones back inside and they would hide them over and over again until finally the eggs were so cracked many were ruined.

We made egg salad and other salads out of the usable eggs and the dogs got the remainder. Always in summer when we mowed the yard we would run the mower over a forgotten egg. How rotten the egg would have smelled by then.

So this Easter are you planning any of the activities we enjoyed as children and young parents? How many are planning to go to church on Easter Sunday? Did you remember to buy the dye kits and extra eggs and a chocolate bunny? If not, get cracking!

The Easter bunny is on his way and there is a church pew with your name on it waiting for you. And don't forget your Easter bonnet.

The Family Community

Years ago being one of eight children born to a farm family was an everyday happening. In fact, to be from a small family back then was rare. It took a bunch of kids to help with all the work on the farm and to feeding all of those mouths.

Living as a member of a large family was like living in a small community. There were leaders and followers, doers and shirkers, bosses and employees. You could be the best friend of one sibling and/or the bane of another. You were either older or younger or somewhere in the middle of the roster, but you never doubted you belonged to that "community."

At our house the "family" consisted of two parents, eight children and one or the other of the grandmothers at nearly all times of the year.

Also back then, divorce was almost unheard of among my friends. All but two or three of the kids I knew were from a firmly established, traditional two-parent family and, like us, many of them had a grandparent present on the scene.

The grandmother wasn't just there because she didn't have a home of her own, at least both of ours did. They just chose to live with us for six months at a time, splitting their time among all their children in the general area enjoying the company of their married child and that child's children.

Like any established society, Mother and Dad's word was law, but following up on that was either Mama Day's or Mama Caudill's law, followed closely by our brother Jim's law. (We always called each of our grandmothers by the title of Mama followed by their last name.)

Most of us never knew either of our grandfathers because they both died long before we were born.

The parents, grandparents or brother Jim also served as the judge, jury and executioner if need be. But any society needs rules to live by I guess.

I think I dreaded Jim's laws worst of all. His rules were much stricter than our parents' and he knew how to enforce them too.

Jim Day

Jim made up rules for our dating young men as we girls got older. The boy must come in the house and speak to the parents for a short while. If our date drove up and just tooted his horn for us to come out, Jim sent them on their way and told them not to return. We could not date anyone from Freetown or Medora because those boys were considered "trouble". In fact, if Jim found any excuse at all to send them away, he sent them. There was no recourse.

Since my Dad often worked out of state on construction jobs of one sort or another, Mother often spent the weekend on a bus trip to visit him, leaving brother Jim in charge. Our three older brothers had all left home by the time I was six or seven years old, leaving Jim as the oldest and consequently the job of baby sitter. We loved to make his life miserable, or at least I did.

I think I had more spankings from Jim than I ever did from a parent. I don't remember ever getting a spanking from either of my grandmothers. They were kind of easy marks if I remember correctly.

Dad's mother, Mama Day, was the strictest but we had more fun with her than with Mama Caudill.

I remember one summer Mama Day spent with us from her Florida home (it supposedly was cooler here) and we girls helped her take a shower. In the winter she lived on a beach in Miami with her rich daughter, Audrey, or alternately in Eastern Kentucky with Dad's youngest sister, Anita and her three children.

We didn't have an inside shower at the time so we improvised. Mama Day was a huge woman and suffered in the heat something fierce. We would stand her out in back of the house and pour buckets of icy cold well water over her. That continued until a neighbor complained to Mother about the view so we strung up sheets to protect the neighbor's sensitivity. We personally did not care that she was naked as a jaybird. Mama Day would scream when the cold water was first poured down her then she would laugh and tell us to do it again and again.

The grandmothers also were in charge of braiding my hair each morning. Since I was the only curly-headed daughter he had Dad insisted my hair be kept long. The easiest method of controlling the curl was to braid it.

Mama Day would seat me on the floor in front of her with her knees pressed against each of my shoulders to hold me in place. She would then brush my hair the requisite 100 strokes then comb and braid it. I had a tender scalp and if I hollered or tried to get away she would whack me sharply on the head with the hairbrush and tell me to hush. When she was finished braiding, my eyes slanted like an

Oriental's because the braids were pulled so tightly but a few hours later the curls would have destroyed the tightest braids and I would look like I had been inside a tornado.

She was a wonderful teller of ghost stories. Every evening as we sat out on the lawn where it was cooler, (there were no air conditioners in those long ago days) she would sit there long into the night, with us kids sitting on a blanket on the ground around her, telling us "haint" tales. By the time we went to bed we were scared to death. I wish now I had recorded some of those stories, but those days were long before the invention of the tape recorder so those stories have been lost forever. I just remember the chills and fear as she related these old time tales to us.

Mama Day standing in her flower garden.

She loved flowers as long as there was a grandchild at hand to do the work of weeding, hoeing, manuring and watering. She also loved bird watching and could get doves to answer her by cooing to them.

She liked to tell us what the hoot owl said. The owl, she told us said, "We cook for ourselves who cooks for you all-l-l-l-l-l?" We believed her. If you listen closely today I think you will agree that is truly what they say.

Mama Caudill, Mother's mom, who lived to be 96, was a gentler sort of woman. She had many talents but, unlike Mama Day who was well read, she could neither read nor write until very late in life. She had never had the opportunity to attend school as a youngster. She learned to read as Mother read children's books we left with her to read to our kids when she baby-sat them.

Mama Caudill was so proud of the fact she could read she was given three or four children's books of her own. She would sit on a stool by the heating stove in the living room with those books tucked under her arm after she had finished reading them. She must have made up for lost time because she read them over and over.

That tall stool by the stove was her favorite place to sit. I guess because it was so warm by the fire and she could watch her johnnie cakes browning in the skillet on top of the stove or in the hot coal-filled ashpan.

To make her johnnie cakes, Mama Caudill would take a cup each of flour and corn meal, 2 teaspoons of baking powder, a pinch of baking soda, salt to taste, add enough buttermilk to make a stiff batter and mix well. Once she had an iron skillet really hot, she would add some bacon drippings or lard and after it melted, drop by tablespoonful the johnnie cake mixture into the hot grease. She would allow it to brown well on the bottom, checking it often, then flip it over and bake the other side until the dough was done in the middle.

You should always eat the johnnie cakes while they are hot and they are delicious if you spread some freshly churned cow butter on it. Mama liked to break hers up in a big glass of buttermilk and eat it like that. She told me they were called johnnie cakes because of the Civil War song, "When Johnnie Comes Marching Home." The soldiers, who were often referred to as Johnny, could bake their own cornbread while on bivouac.

A lot of times she would also be roasting herself some yellow yams on top of the stove to go along with her johnnie cakes. The heating stove heated her and the food she liked to eat at the same time. Once the cornbread and the yams were done, she would place them on a small plate and smear them liberally with the rich butter from the farm.

Mama Caudill was a tough old bird. After falling and breaking her leg when she was in her mid 70s the doctors told her she would probably never walk again. She stayed with us until the cast came off and within about six months she was walking again without crutches and she returned to her own home for many active years to come. She often referred to doctors as "those old fools," saying they "didn't know what they were talking about." I think I agree with her to some extent as they have treated me pretty shabbily over the years.

When Mama Caudill wasn't living with us she lived alone in a tiny crude cabin in the mountains of Eastern Kentucky, right behind the house where another daughter and her husband lived. It was there on Pine Mountain that she loved to hunt for squirrels with her old Kentucky long rifle. On these walks through her beloved mountains she would take an old gunnysack with her and place inside it small dry twigs she picked up in her wanderings. When she returned home the twigs would be spread out under her house's porch inside a screened wire container placed there by her son-in-law Clarence. This would provide her with kindling with which to start her fires in the wintertime. Heavier wood would be cut and stacked to supplement her efforts once the fire was started.

One day when she was 92 and was returning from a hunting foray Mama Caudill accidentally stepped on her cat's tail as it was lying on her house step. When the cat jumped away, it threw Mama Caudill down and she broke her hip.

After two hip replacement surgeries failed she had to be admitted to a nursing home where she died at age 96. Even at that great age, Mama was still not totally gray headed; she still had some dark streaks in her long hair.

The funniest thing I remember about Mama Caudill had to do with man's stepping on the moon for the first time. Mama flatly did not believe me when I told her during a visit with my young family and said, "'pon my honor, Helen, if they had done that they would have put its little light out."

Mama Caudill, Mother and Sylvia at the nursing home where she resided for four years.

And so it was with many other of our modern day inventions for Mama Caudill.

As a young woman she had helped her husband farm and raise an orchard and big gardens and several kids. She related to us how she would load her produce in panniers on the sides of her mule or horse and ride down to the town of Whitesburg. While there she would sell her produce or barter for the essentials she needed for her family.

Living to this great age can be a disadvantage. If you are in your 90s, then most likely your children are well advanced in years also and may be physically unable to care for you themselves in their home or you need more care than they are trained to give. Probably all your friends and family members are already dead also. You begin to live an isolated existence except for your immediate family. That was the case with Mama Caudill.

I still think with a great deal of love of these two old women, Mama Day and Mama Caudill, and think about all they gave of themselves to us and how times have changed, and maybe not for the better either. I like to think I also remember some of their lessons to us kids.

It was so much fun, having three generations living in one household. I loved hearing their stories and lore about their childhood and their own young days as a married woman. Each of these women were able to spend time in their children's homes, taking care of the women as they gave birth to her grandchildren, often assisting at the birth themselves, helping raise those grandchildren, telling the kids big yarns and adding so much color and love to their lives.

Today few if any grandparents are present in the homes of their children and grandchildren. The elderly are often shuffled off to nursing homes as soon as they begin to fail. How sad it is that some grandchildren hardly even know their grandparents or think of them as just that old man or woman they go to the nursing home to visit.

And it is just as lonely an existence for the old person. If you do not believe me, borrow a child to take with you on a visit to a nursing home. That child will be bombarded from all sides with women and men anxious to make contact with a young child. The oldsters long to touch, hear and feel the faces of the children one more time. It is heartbreaking sometimes to see this. It can be traumatic for the child if it has not been accustomed to visiting the elderly.

I don't feel it's always neglect by their children necessarily that this happens. In many instances their children are still busily working at jobs to support not only themselves, but also many times to support their own grandchildren, these older people's great-grandchildren.

All too often today, grandparents are raising grandchildren because the children are victims of a broken home, drug and alcohol abuse or simply of inadequate parenting.

It is a rare fact indeed when you hear of couples being married a great number of years. Might it not be a blessing to us all to step back and be able to run our homes as the ones in our childhood were run? Throw in the parents, grandparents, grandchildren, cats and dogs, add a lot of love, mix well and enjoy.

I might even agree to obey brother Jim's rules. He is still alive after all. In fact, all of our eight siblings still are living and we range in age from 58 to 74 and are scattered over a large part of the United States. A few are beginning to fail physically, but we are still able to enjoy visiting each other and recalling the past.

My Turn at Motherhood

I sure had a lot still to learn when it became my turn to become a young wife and mother. As I have explained in another chapter, I could not cook anything at all when I married except for being able to bake a skillet of cornbread. Everything else was beyond my abilities. I had never been a babysitter or made a house a home, so I had not acquired any of those skills. I had never made a cookie except for trying it one time and failing miserably when I used fly spray instead of Wesson Oil, but that is another long story. To be really honest, I was a total amateur at life and living.

My husband, Mickey, and Me on our wedding day, March 6, 1960 in Seymour, Indiana.

I could milk a cow and churn butter or cut, split and set a fence post and stretch the fence to hold the cow inside, but I did not know how to do much else. Oh, I have always been able to type words on paper at a terrific rate and tell a passable story or take shorthand, but when it came to working in a home and raising kids I was passed over.

I never understood how Mother could have given birth to eight children, mended their broken bones, stitched up their cuts and sent them on their way with only a bottle of liquid Lysol, hot water and soap. Where were her tranquilizers? And at the end of every day she would be bathed, freshly dressed and ready to greet Dad at the front door. By my day's end, I looked like I had just endured a full-blown hurricane I was so frazzled. Maybe it was just a more difficult endeavor when my two sons were born. And let me tell you a secret, having two kids is enough for any mother.

First of all somewhere along the line they came to me defective. There was no Owner's Manual, Repair Book or Parts List issued to me at the hospital where they were both born. Neither was there a money back guarantee. Was this something a grandmother passed down to her daughter and granddaughters? If so, it completely skipped me somehow. Like being a good cook skipped me.

For the first fifteen years or so of my married life when Mother planned her frequent reunions, I would be asked to bring a loaf of bread or bag of potato chips. Likewise, I could bring the paper plates and plastic silverware. Anything was acceptable from me except the food that would have had to come from my kitchen. There were all afraid of it. When my newspaper editor named me cooking editor Mother was really scared. She told me, "Helen you could actually kill somebody, be really careful." This from my own mother whom I had always loved and trusted.

When I held my first son in my arms for the very first time at the hospital, I had just taken a bath and put on a new gown. I had slept through his birth due to the drugs they gave me so I was ready to see this tiny scrap of humanity and make sure all the parts were included. He was so ugly I was ready to give him back. His head was misshapen and covered with light fuzz that stuck straight out about an inch long—he looked like he had been electrocuted; his blue eyes were not focused, his neck was pretty wobbly and he was hungry. The hungry part stays with him to this very day. Fortunately the rest of him got much better with age. Further, by the time I took him home five days later he was completely bald for some reason and would stay that way for a number of years. This may explain his skimpy hairline today. Did that portend his future?

I eagerly accepted him into my loving arms. He was wrapped in a soft blue blanket and that helped a bit to make him more attractive. The nurse handed me a bottle filled with milk which I promptly fed to him, all of it. What an ungrateful baby he was! Within five minutes of inhaling the whole bottle of milk he "spit up" the entire bottle all at once and all over my new gown. Erupted would be a better term for what he did to me. There must have been a quart of milk in that little four-ounce bottle. No way could what was on my gown have been only four ounces. No one had explained the term "burping" to me. I didn't realize he was swallowing as much air as milk and you had to stop occasionally and expel the air. My husband tells our grandson that his dad was the only kid he ever saw who was born with a full set of teeth. Each tooth and ounce of flesh would cost us thousands of dollars in repairs and food bills.

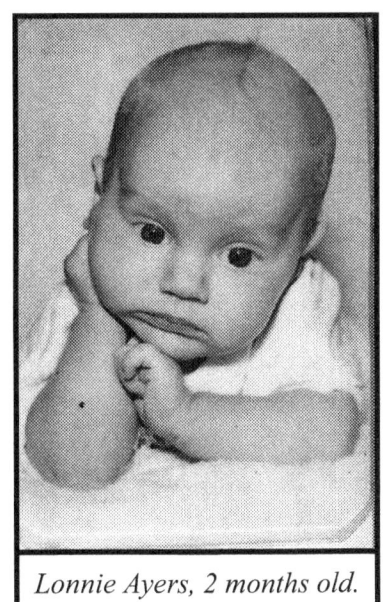
Lonnie Ayers, 2 months old.

That was just for starters! He then proceeded to strain and grunt and turn red in the face. Pretty soon I figured out what was going on at his other end. Gross. What was this? I wondered. Did I need to diaper both ends of him? You fill one end and let it fall out the other? What a waste that seemed.

Truly, I was just about that dumb. I think every baby should arrive with its own user's guide under one arm, especially if every new mom is as green as I was.

Five days after his birth they told me to take him home. Were they kidding me? That wasn't part of the deal. Didn't I even get to negotiate? "Nope," they said, 'Just take him home and do the best you can."

I let them wheel me down the hall to the elevator, talking to the Big Guy all the way. "Thanks, Big Guy, You've really done it to me this time."

I know I heard a big deep gruff laugh which sounded just like the Jolly Green Giant in the television commercials and I know he patted me on the head as he told me to "have a jolly, ho, ho, good time."

Me, Mickey and a young Lonnie

The Big Guy has a really droll sense of humor if He expected me to go for it. I didn't have a clue what I needed to do for this tiny piece of humanity. Do babies break easy? "No," he assured me, they were pretty tough, "but be careful with him." What do you do if they cry and won't stop? "Why, you feed them of course," I didn't know anything about this new career but I would quickly learn what he meant by "feed them."

We never knew what a leftover was until he graduated and left for the Air Force. It took me a while to learn to cook for three instead of six, excuse me, four—it just seemed like six I had fed him for so long.

They sent him home with me with instructions on how to feed and bathe him. It would take me six weeks to be able to bathe him without him turning blue and shaking feverishly. How do you get one squirming kid wet all over and not freeze him to death, was one big question I had. My sister-in-law, Roy's wife Dorothy, showed me how to put his whole body into a pan of water all at once, slosh the soapy water gently over him, then remove the baby from the water and towel him dry. You were supposed to throw the bath water out and keep the baby, Dorothy explained to me. There were times I was tempted I can tell you. But bathing the baby this way made things much easier for both of us. I just needed three or four hands to keep his head above the water level and wash him at the same time without his slick squirming body squirting out from between my fingers like a seed from an orange.

Mother liked for me to bring him to her house and leave him for the weekend whenever I wanted a break, and boy did I need a break on a regular basis; he practically lived at her place that first year. Thank God for Grandmas. She is the one who recognized he needed to see a doctor when he was four months old because he had pneumonia. I thought he merely had a cold.

At about nine months of age he was climbing and walking and slid through a slatted bench and caught his head between the slats of the bench at the laundromat. I spent the next two hours at the hospital getting the first of his stitches applied. I should have had them make a pretty design with tattoo ink each time they had to sew him up which was frequently. His life could have been much more exciting when he explained to someone what this design or that design was caused by. And if I had saved all the casts from his broken bones, I would have had to rent a U-Haul to store them in. That was one sorry kid I can tell you.

By the time my second son was born twenty-eight months later I felt like an old pro. I had this motherhood business down pretty pat I thought. Dream on lady I found out. This is when I found out that every child is different and each has different problems.

The Big Guy Upstairs had a second surprise for me. Just when I had the first one paper and litterbox trained, he sent me another to work on. What a sense of humor he had. I'm sure he's still laughing about this joke.

The second son was born with a hernia in his right groin and had to have surgery when he was only 18 months old to repair it. I knew he was going to be real trouble before he was ever born. I was admitted to the hospital with false labor five times before he finally arrived on the very day the doctor had originally told me he would arrive. I should have known he would be extra trouble.

Picture of me holding baby and hugging older son.

Doug was also born with a propensity to incur head injuries which lead to brain concussions which led to near fatal attacks by his poor mother. This kid literally scared me to death on a frequent basis. By the time he was in the fifth grade of school he had already received the last of his six brain concussions.

On concussion number five I think it was, as we drove to the hospital with him in my arms, wrapped in a blanket, windows rolled up and the heater going full blast to warm his cold body in mid-August in Indiana, he awoke long enough to ask, "Am I going to die this time Mom?" He shivered. No, I assured him, but I just might.

There is absolutely no way on this earth I could have stitched him up, operated on him, set his bones, or done any of the things Mother had done for us using only liquid Lysol, warm water and soap. My two kids needed to belong to a medical doctor's family.

I have often wondered how she could have patched up eight of us. No wonder I already have more gray hair than Mother ever had.

When I wanted to talk to our boys and they were outside, I had to look to the tops of the trees surrounding our lawn and see which one was shaking the worst. The shaking meant they were at the top of that tree having a good time. With a Tarzan-like yell they would swing from limb to limb and come down to the ground to see what I needed.

My husband and I taught the boys many things like how to butcher a hog, make maple syrup from tree sap, snare a fish, and many other useful things. One thing I'm not too sure about teaching them though is about honesty. Both can tell some pretty good tales.

Lonnie loves to tell how he caught a big bass and how an even bigger one grabbed the smaller one just as he was ready to pull it out of the water on to the bank of a pond. The bigger of the two fish weighed about five pounds and the smaller one about two pounds when he got them ashore. Sure sounds like a fish story to me.

Doug, thankfully, did not share Lonnie's ability to tell fish stories.

But as much trouble as my kids were with their many injuries, they were a joy to finally get to adulthood in one piece. They never drank alcohol, smoked cigarettes, used drugs, cursed me or others. They were always kind to, and loved visiting with, their grandparents and the many other elderly people of their acquaintance. They were both named Hoosier scholars in high school, excelled in Little League baseball, and took music lessons.

Picture of Lonnie and his bass.

Lonnie's high school graduation picture

Doug's high school graduation picture.

Upon reaching college age they did just as well. Both now have their MBA degrees from good colleges and travel the world assisting global sized companies with their problems. Both are looking forward to getting their doctorates some day. They will need them to keep ahead of their Mom.

I have never told them that I finally learned how to make cookies. For their entire lives I had them convinced there were only two kinds of people who could bake cookies. That included their Aunt Sandra and the Keebler elves.

I guess I showed those two guys.

And the Big Guy's reaction to my child rearing abilities? He patted me on the head again and said, "Well done. Ho, Ho. Ho."

This is Lonnie, (L) and Douglas with their wives, Koyoko (Doug's) and Conchita at Doug's commencement from the Indiana Institute of Technology in 1985.

Hobos and the Train

Growing up in a small town back in the good old days could be either dull and boring or as exciting as you wanted to make it. Most of the time I preferred to make it exciting and I still look at the world through rose-colored glasses my sons and friends tell me.

One of the greatest entertainments for any kid back in the 1940s and 50s was when the steam train came through the town of Kurtz. The Chicago, Milwaukee and St. Paul made two trips through town each day.

When the steam locomotive left Freetown to the East and started towards Kurtz four miles away at a steady chug-chug we could see the steam pouring from its stacks a long way off. This gave us time to run or bicycle the three blocks across town so we would be in place to wave to the engineer and brakeman. They probably knew each kid on sight along the train's entire run.

There was a tall water tower standing on the back street side of Kurtz under which the train would stop each way and take on water to make steam. This would usually take a few minutes and give the kids a chance to really look the train and its loads over.

The engine would be kept running so the vibrations were still there and you could feel them from a goodly way off. Some of the really brave kids would scamper underneath the train from side to side until the whistle blew for the train to leave but I never had the nerve to do that.

It would also give the hobos, and there were many in the earlier years we lived in Kurtz, a chance to jump from the freight cars like rats deserting a sinking ship. While the train was stopped taking on water, the hobos would come out from under the car's suspension or out of the sliding doors of the cars and take off across town at a run.

When they jumped off during the night run, they could be found on our doorstep next morning eating their breakfasts. Mother always rose early and made a huge breakfast for our large family. Usually there was enough left over to feed several others and the food never went to waste. I don't know how the hobos had marked our farmhouse but they surely did. There were always hobos to be fed and I remember waking several times and looking out our bedroom window toward the porch, seeing all these strange often dirty looking men sitting there eating and talking among themselves.

The food might not have been what they particularly wanted that morning, but it would be clean, well prepared and nutritious. Mother made the best biscuits I ever ate.

I don't know where the hobos slept as they waited the night out for the train to return from the other direction. Perhaps they found our haymows warm and comfortable. We were so tired we always went to bed very early so I never discovered where the hobos slept. By the time it was dark, we were sacked out in our good warm beds.

By the time the morning freight had stopped to take on water, the hobos would have been fed. They would sneak (I think the trainmen felt sorry for them and allowed them to sneak) back inside the cars for their return journey to wherever they came from or were going to.

The hobos never presented a problem to us and Mother never turned anyone away from her table hungry. Many insisted on helping her in return for the food. Most times she would permit them to split some firewood for her woodburner in the kitchen she used for cooking our meals. The hobos would sing to the cadence of their chopping and their efforts took some of the work off us kids.

The steam train was truly huge and it was tremendous and wonderful and glorious.

Sometimes some of the older boys would stand outside on a tiny platform on the trestle over Salt Creek and they would be very close to the train as it was coming to a stop. The noise and the vibrations were enough to scare me so I never tried that trick.

Just under the trestle was a fairly deep hole of water where every kid in town swam during hot weather. Usually the engineer would expel his excess steam and soot as he crossed the trestle above us spraying it onto us in the water and waving to us kids as he left.

I remember one time passenger cars were sidetracked to a spur in Kurtz to be living quarters for those men who were repairing the tracks.

The trainmen invited all the kids in the neighborhood to come inside to see how they lived. There were bunks stacked on each side of the cars and each man had a trunk in which his clothes were stored. Another car was a dining car where they shared meals. There was a wood stove in each car for heat and for heating hot water to bathe.

I don't know if I remember when the train carried passengers or if I have just heard of it so often that I think I remember. Anyway, there was a hotel in Norman, four miles to the west of Kurtz to serve those passengers who wished to depart the train for awhile.

We had moved to Kurtz in the fall of 1948 and it may be there were no passengers carried after that time. I can only remember the freight cars.

One time I was riding Jimmy's bicycle down the main artery through Kurtz toward the train track. As I passed the grocery store which sat right next to the railroad tracks, everyone starting hollering at me and waving their arms. I didn't know what they were saying because I could not hear them for the noise. It finally dawned on me I guess that the train was coming. I looked to the west and there it was, huge, nearly at the crossing, its brakes screaming and its whistle blowing frantically. I guess at me. I immediately dropped the bike down onto the pavement and scratched my legs up badly. A second or so later and I would have been on the track. That was what the people at the store were trying to tell me, that the train was there and for some reason I was not hearing it.

Many of the trains were very long and very heavy.

Between Kurtz and Norman there was a long, fairly steep grade. At times half the train cars would have to be unhitched and part of the train taken on to Norman and sidetracked on a spur located there for loading timber and crossties. Then the locomotive would reverse back down the hill to pull the other cars up over the grade. There was always a kid at Norman begging the trainman to let them ride in the cab with them to go get the other half of the train. They wanted to blow that whistle and feel that vibration up close and personal. And I'm sure even though it was against the rules, many of those kids got to ride that train free. How exciting that would have been.

I remember lying in bed hearing the coupling and straining of the big train engines far into the night when sleep eluded me. There isn't a kid alive who could resist the allure of the steam locomotive.

The husband of one of our neighbors worked on a train but had to drive to Bedford to get on it. The wife had a boyfriend whose company she had enjoyed for many years. Once her husband left for work, she would turn her porch light on. When her boyfriend drove slowly by her house, if he saw the porch light on he knew the coast was clear and stopped and stayed a few hours. If the porch light was not on, he would speed up and drive away.

It was many years before someone told the husband about the boyfriend visiting his wife. One night the husband pretended to go to work and drove away. The porch light came on and the boyfriend stopped and went inside. The husband returned and caught the guilty party inside together. The boyfriend bailed out, jumped into his car and sped away. The wife would not let her husband inside the house because she knew he would beat her up. As he ran around the house to attempt to get in at another doorway, she would shoot a pistol through the window or door glass.

The next day the husband and wife had reconciled and he asked Dad if he would come over and replace the glass panes. There were nine panes of glass shot out the previous night. That fight did not stop the shenanigans, but it was the only time I can remember that he caught her in the act. Their fights were numerous and greatly entertaining and loud. We kids enjoyed watching and listening to them. Their fights were as entertaining as seeing a movie.

This same neighbor was one of the first to own a television set in the little town. We were still years away from owning one ourselves and used to sit on a quilt on our lawn and watch the test pattern intently until we heard the N B C chimes. She would sometimes let us kids come into the house and watch with her for an hour or so. At that time the networks were only on the air with programming for about four hours total. When programming stopped, the test pattern would be on for hours until it was time for the next show to start. But if she left it playing test patterns, we sat right there on our lawn and watched it. We didn't care because it was still exciting to see this activity coming over the airwaves into the pretty box. How naïve we were at that time.

Sometime in the 1950s the steam locomotive met its demise and diesel power took over. It was never quite the same after that. There was just something mysterious and exciting about seeing those great puffs of steam from the smoke stacks floating away behind the caboose, listening to the whistle blowing and feeling the ground vibrating under your feet.

In the 1970s even the diesel train stopped running through Kurtz. On its last ride through town, it pulled up its rails and tracks and moved on. If you watch closely even today as you travel State Road 58 from State Road 135 south of Freetown west to Bedford you can see where the tracks once lay.

When we went to Bedford to visit our optometrist or to shop, we would cross the track or go under a trestle 13 times between Kurtz and Bedford.

The great steam locomotives are now long gone. I'm glad it is in my memory to enjoy forever.

Three Witches

Most people do not believe in witches, but I certainly do. If the period I grew up in had been during the Salem Witch Trials, I probably would have been in the docks or burned at the stake along with my mother and grandmother. All three of us were witches but we always used our talents for the benefit of those around us, never for evil purposes and each of us had a separate distinct talent.

My Mama Caudill was able to soothe a bad burn by "blowing the fire out" as she would describe it. She did it for me when a kettle of hot vegetable soup exploded and fell onto the right side of my body. She was present and blew softly over the burned area as she uttered unheard words under her breath. With all that heat in my body I should have been blistered badly or even deformed by scar tissue. I didn't have even a single blister and within an hour you could not even tell I had had an accident.

Mother, in her turn, was able to witch warts from people. And there was one very special story about that.

When she witched warts she would tell the person having one to pick up a small round stone about the size of a coin and rub it on their wart. They would then be advised to tie that "coin" inside one corner of a white handkerchief and drop the whole thing where someone else would be sure to find it, like on a busy street somewhere. When the finder picked it up, thinking a woman had lost her handkerchief that she kept her coins in, as was the custom in those days, the wart would transfer to the finder. That was the theory at least.

One day a woman came to our house. She was the daughter of a neighbor and was reputed to be a former madam in a house of ill repute in a nearby town. She recently had fallen on hard times and had come to live with her mother along with six or seven of her children.

When she came to our house in great distress one day she was dressed in a white silk blouse and really pretty white twill shorts showing off a lot of very long tanned leg. On her feet were white leather strappy sandals and her hair was swept up into a beautiful bouffant hairdo. The most remarkable aspect of her appearance though was a huge grainy wart on the side of her nose that had suddenly appeared.

She was so distressed Mother started asking her questions such as "How long have you had it?" Turned out she had had the ugly wart only a few days.

She then proceeded to tell Mother about finding a flat stone in a handkerchief and Mother remembered witching a wart from Sylvia's finger. Dorothy had picked up the handkerchief Sylvia had dropped in the edge of our driveway and had gotten Sylvia's wart which had disappeared, never to appear again on Sylvia. It had a new home.

Abashed and amused at the same time, Mother told Dorothy about witching warts and the woman got furious. She jumped up from the living room sofa and ran screaming out of our house yelling epithets against Mother and her witching powers as she went.

Sylvia had been mopping the kitchen floor prior to Dorothy's arrival. When finished, she had taken the bucket of dirty mop water out into the yard and left it there to empty and rinse the mop later on after the floor had dried.

As Dorothy ran screaming and crying from the house, she accidentally planted her dainty little shod foot into the bucket of dirty mop water. She lost her balance and fell headlong into the yard knocking the bucket over and spilling the mop water all over her body and nice clothes, effectively ruining her silk shirt.

Picking herself up from the lawn, by this time she was hysterical, she ran to her Mother's house. A few days later she moved out bag and baggage from her Mother's house and we never saw her or her wart ever again. I think her mother was please she had gone.

When our son, Lonnie was young he had a huge ugly wart on top of the middle finger of his right hand. He was always knocking it loose and making it bleed when he was working and playing. I took him to our family doctor twice and had it surgically removed. On the third trip to do this there was a much older doctor visiting his friend that day. He picked up Lonnie's hand, looked at the wart and rubbed one of his fingers over it. He told our doctor, "I don't think you need to take this off again, I think it will be OK now." A few days later it disappeared, never to return

Was this learned older doctor a witch doctor? Perhaps he was. Or did I just believe in the power of "witching?"

My witching abilities enable me to find underground water and other cavities underground such as lost septic tanks. If someone needs a well witched, I can do that. If they move to a new home and don't know where the septic tank is located I can find it. I have found water where dozens of others have failed and more of it than many hoped to ever find when they paid a well driller to come onto their property.

I did not know for many years that I could do this. My husband was a water well driller most of his life and he generally witched before drilling. One day he asked me to try and handed me his wires which did not work at all for me. He then cut me a forked dogwood stick and asked me to try that. I did and when I walked over an area, it immediately bend down and nearly tore the skin from my hands. That was the first indication I had that I, too, might be a witch.

We did not get that job, but on the way home he asked me to witch a well for his brother who had tried seven times without success to have a well drilled on his house lot.

I very easily found that my stick went down. Mickey drilled where I said and got worlds of water. The brother then had a driller who drilled only large diameter wells to come and drill where we had and he never again lacked for water.

An older gentleman boss I had at the Job Corps Center where I worked heard about my witching water. He could not do it himself but knew immediately after I rearranged his office furniture that something was wrong. Nothing would make him shut up until I brought my dogwood stick into his office and witched for water. I had placed his desk over a water main under the floor and it had been making him antsy.

We rearranged the furniture away from the water main and he was then fine.

Mickey can witch with copper wires, usually coat hangers that have been straightened then bent at an angle with one long and one very short side. He would hold the short ends in his hands and walk first north and south, then east and west. Where the two lines intersected is where he would drill. He believed that would give him the possibility of striking water at two levels, one stream moving north and south; the other moving from east to west, usually at different depths. I, and both our sons, can witch for water using the forked dogwood stick, but none of us can tell you how far below the surface the water level is. Only drilling tells us that.

So I know Mother's wart witching tricks and I can use forked sticks and witch for water, but I never got to learn Mama Caudill's secret of blowing fire from burns.

I asked her one time what she was saying under her breath when she was performing her magic on me and she told me that if she taught me how to do it she would never be able to do it

Lonnie and Mickey witching.

again herself. She could only teach it to a non-relative. If I had had the sense of a goose I should have asked her to teach it to someone I knew who could have then taught it back to me. But there may have been a prohibition against this route too, I do not know.

I was at a friend's restaurant a couple of years ago when she was burned badly on her right hand and lower arm as she attempted to empty her grill's grease container and the hot grease slopped out on her arm and hand.

I had just walked in and saw her lividly red arm inside a clean garbage sack filled with ice to relieve some of the pain. She was in true agony and I asked if I could drive her to the emergency room. She got this bright idea look on her face and instead went to the telephone and called a friend, a "fire witch". She explained to him what had happened and how painful and red it was. He told her he could not come there right then but told her he felt she would be OK even if he didn't show up.

Fifteen minutes or so later she removed her now normal looking arm from the bag of ice and calmly went into the cleanup area of her restaurant and plunged her arms down into the hot soapy dishwater and was serenely washing the day's dishes without a sign of pain on her face.

"I told you he could remove the fire," she laughingly told me.

The Turkey

Christmas is just around the corner again and it reminds me of when my Mother went on strike one Christmas against the grocery stores because of their high turkey prices.

"I will not pay those prices," she was heard to say several times. "I'll just buy me a live turkey and clean it myself and save a bunch of money."

She may have saved money, but she nearly lost her religion trying to pluck it.

Now Mother was a very proficient farm wife and had butchered hundreds of chickens in her prime, but she had never cleaned a turkey.

So about a week before the Christmas holiday, sometime in the mid 1950's, she went to a turkey farm and bought a 30 pound tom turkey and locked him in the hen house until a day or so before the holiday.

Turkeys had always come to our table via the grocery store in bags with their neck and other unmentionables stuffed inside them leaving a very attractive hunk of meat to look at and cook.

That huge turkey would be the first, one and only, and last live turkey she would ever fool with. And it sure was ugly. It had awful colors on its head and a long beard out of its chest, and it was nearly grotesque. How something that ugly could be so pretty and taste so good roasted and stuffed with goodies is still a mystery I don't understand.

Early morning on turkey butchering day Mother had one of my brothers chop the turkey's head off while she got the fire going under the 55-gallon barrel of water into which she was going to dunk him. Supposedly dunking one into very hot water will make the feathers come right out. At least that is what she thought. It was a fowl wasn't it and a chicken was a fowl and that is the way she always prepared them, so bring on the tom turkey.

First she learned it was too heavy for her to handle alone, and even too heavy for whichever of her many sons was helping her, so they rigged up a rope and pulley system.

They would dunk the turkey for what they thought was a reasonable amount of time then pull on the rope and tie it off. My brother would have walked away at that time, leaving Mother to her job.

She valiantly did her best to pull those feathers out the same way she would have done a chicken, but the job was just bigger than she was.

She called for my brother to help again. He dunked the turkey again and she tried pulling those feathers out but finally she had to call a halt.

Dad and us kids had been watching the action out the kitchen window and wondered just how long Mother would keep to the task before she called for reinforcements or threw the turkey to the pigs and asked Dad to go to town and buy one.

Dad finally took her a pair of pliers and helped her pull each feather out individually and then helped her singe the remaining pinfeathers from the bird. Handling a 30-pound turkey was far different than lifting and handling a five-pound chicken.

After carrying it into the house and washing it thoroughly and removing the innards, she stuffed him full of the most succulent cornbread dressing and stuck him in the oven to bake.

If I remember correctly, it tasted pretty good. I am sure by that time that it was a beautiful golden brown from stem to stern. At our house with ten hungry family members and a host of relatives around the table it would have been cleaned from the bone in minutes whether it tasted like shoe leather or not.

Mother dared anyone to ask one question about that turkey but later she said she would pay whatever price the stores wanted and would never try that again.

Disasters like that one can ruin any holiday, as I would find out twenty some years ago when a friend and I decided to cook a Thanksgiving dinner and serve anyone who would come and eat with us.

This turned out to be a good idea in the end but that first one was a mind-boggler for sure.

You see, I was never a good cook and I had never cooked a turkey myself when I made this momentous decision.

That year it was just my husband, younger son and myself to eat so I came up with the idea and shared it with an EMT friend who would have had only himself, wife and two very young children at his table.

"It is silly for each of us to cook, or anyone else for that matter, when there are so few in the family," we said to each other.

So we advertised the dinner in the local paper and people from all walks of life sent us money to buy things we needed or gave us items to cook.

A local chef loaned us his kitchen to use and met with us to help plan the meal. He asked, "How do you prepare your turkey and how many are you planning to serve?"

My friend and I looked at each other and said we didn't know how many we were planning to serve since we had asked everyone to eat with us who wanted to do so. I timidly said I had never cooked a turkey before. As to how many we would cook, that would depend on how many were donated, we told him.

He was aghast, but said he would train us quickly and loan us his kitchen so we went blindly ahead. This was the experience that would prove to us there are guardian angels watching over ignorant people.

Mark and I ended up cooking 23 turkeys because that's how many were donated.

Chef Ramón asked if I knew how to make gravy and I said I could make it two cups at a time and he promptly told me I would need gallons of it. I nearly froze.

A volunteer who had once owned a restaurant showed up who knew how to make gravy, in volume, so that problem vanished.

I did make the dressing because I could do that by this time in my life.

Chef Ramón told us we would need at least 69 pies. We had none when we left the restaurant the night before Thanksgiving.

But faith plays a large part in this story. The next morning, very early my husband and I drove to the restaurant and there on tables were literally hundreds of slices of pies on small paper plates each covered with plastic wrap. The churchwomen had come through for us and delivered the pies during the night.

There were probably 18 people sleeping in the lobby on couches, chairs or in sleeping bags on the floor who had worked on the meal all night. Others had cleaned the kitchen which had had over 600 meals cooked in it the weekend before but no dishes had been done.

One volunteer had worked for many years as a dishwasher in a restaurant's kitchen using that same kind of equipment. He was a real lifesaver and worked all that day leaving that kitchen spotless. He was a real angel in disguise.

The green beans and sweet potatoes were no problem, either of us could cook those, but we had kind of a small spat over who needed the onions worse, him for his beans or I for the dressing. We finally agreed to share them but I got even and made Mark do the chopping.

Even Santa made an appearance and everyone attending the dinner was given a treat furnished free by a candy store in town. Another business had donated a Christmas tree to use and a third store had donated almost a thousand decorations.

Picture of me with Santa at our first Thanksgiving.

People actually insisted on leaving a donation for what they had eaten and we ended up collecting about $900 over and above what we needed so we donated all of it to a local children's Christmas auction.

This year a newer group of EMTs continued the tradition of serving a free Thanksgiving dinner to anyone who wanted to eat. To date the EMTs have donated over $20,000 to the children's Christmas auction from this free Thanksgiving meal idea of mine.

I know this has nothing to do with the Christmas season because we began this tradition for Thanksgiving, but it started with me trying to find a way, like Mother, around a big turkey problem.

Summertime Chores

Well it's summer time and the living is easy. Right? Wrong.

School is out, family vacations are beginning and being stuck inside a car with moaning, complaining kids kicking you in the back of your seat for several hours is enough to turn family planning into reality.

At our house, when I was a kid, summer meant an entirely different thing. It was true that school was out. It was also 100 degrees in the shade and a huge garden was starting to produce prodigious amounts of fresh vegetables. Berries and fruit needed picking and canning. Bugs needed to be plucked from the potato plants and dropped into kerosene. There was always something to be done.

And guess who got to pick, dig or otherwise gather that produce. Kids, of course. I hated that job. All of us had scabs everywhere on our body from gathering this produce. If it itched, we scratched it and suffered the consequences, therefore the scabs and scars of childhood.

Many of the plants in the garden, namely okra, beans and corn and a few others had those despised serrated leaves with prickly spines that itched you to death. Pick a bushel of green beans and I guarantee you would have a bushel of itchy places and chiggers under your skin.

Or pull a couple dozen ears of delicious sweet corn and your bare legs and feet would be covered with scratches from the sharp leaves.

Gardening was not only a chore for the kids it was a necessity if you wanted to eat regularly throughout the rest of the year. Besides that it kept us busy and out of mischief.

First there was the planting of seeds and plants, then hoeing and weeding, then picking, shucking, stringing or stripping in some other manner to prepare the vegetables for canning and freezing or drying.

We made several strings of "shucky beans" every summer. To make these items you needed some extra heavy cord and a darning needle and about a bushel or two of stringed but not broken green beans. To start you needed to push the needle through one bean and tie the string all around it to keep the rest from falling off while you worked

Keep adding beans until you have a pretty good string, maybe 3 feet long. Tie the two ends together to make a loop. Every morning for about a week, place these strings of beans over the clothesline in the direct sun, bringing them inside each night to keep the dew off them, until they are completely dry. Then place them inside a white feed sack and hang them in a closet or the smokehouse. To cook them, place the beans in a large kettle, add sufficient cold water and cook until tender, this usually required several hours cooking. Check them often because as the dried beans rehydrate they will absorb lots of water. You can add jowl bacon and some extra fat and salt to taste when you check them and cut and pull the string out. Some of the Hoosiers we met made these strings of dried green beans, but they called them "leather britches."

Then you would spend hours in a hot kitchen or a table in the back yard canning and freezing the produce. It seemed the chores were never ending in the summer.

If you had a few minutes in which to get into trouble, the garden was a fine spot to work off your demerits. Something always needed doing. "Busy hands" was a motto our mother and grandmothers believed in with gusto.

Fight with a sibling? Snarl at a parent? Decline to do an assigned task? Go directly to the garden. Do not pass the pond and take a warm soothing swim. There was no Get out of jail free card in our family. If you did the deed, you did the time.

But we ate well year round. Just look at any of us eight kids now. We were never near starvation in our lives.

There was a one-legged neighbor who had a strawberry patch. That made a fine place to hide out in the foxtail weeds and eat berries till your belly nearly popped as long as you took him some and brought enough home for a batch of jam or a strawberry pie.

Another man, who mother hired along with his team of horses to cultivate our garden (there were no roto-tillers in those days), had a grape arbor. That was another taste treat as long as we brought home a bushel or two or three for jelly making. There just isn't a better grape in the world than the old dark blue grape.

Mother would make jellies and jams or pies from any fruit or berry, or cooked any meat brought through the door. She always made some jelly up when the produce was brought home to enjoy immediately as a reward for bringing it home. Any extra juices would be canned in jars then made into jelly in the wintertime when we needed the moisture and the heat in the house. Mother might make 20 or 30 jars at a time. To seal them after they had jelled, she would melt paraffin in a pan and pour it over the top inside the jars. Then she would apply a ring and cap to complete the seal.

We could also climb a tree in the fall and harvest fox grapes for jellies. With ten members eating jelly for breakfast, it took several jars of it to last from one season to the next.

If we were in Mother's bad graces we knew we could always get back to a firm footing with her if we cadged some apples from someone's trees for pies. And the man who sold peaches would pull into our driveway sometime during July or August, knowing Mother was a good buyer. Every one of us enjoyed ripe peaches. With that many kids eating pies and jellies I have no idea why we didn't have our own small orchard. We had plenty of space on the farm for one, but I guess the fruits were so plentiful everywhere and everyone who had them shared with all, that we didn't really need one.

Peaches are a fruit fit for the gods. To be good and totally appreciated a ripe, juicy peach should be wiped on your britches leg and eaten on the spot, slightly dusty and fuzzy. The nectar should run down your arm and drip from your elbow and down from your chin and drip onto your chest. MMMMMMM Good. There is no better fruit in my own opinion than a fresh peach.

I remember one time Dad was removing a creosote splinter from between my left big toe and the one next to it that I had picked up while playing on the railroad tracks barefoot, when the peach seller came by. After hollering like a stuck pig while he removed the splinter with a sharp pocketknife, he gave me a couple of fresh peaches to stop my wails.

To this day a fresh peach is my favorite fruit. I will drive for miles to an orchard to get one sun kissed and juicy peach directly from a tree.

We also collected watermelons and cantaloupes from Brownstown and Vallonia each fall. Jackson County melons would be known for their flavor across the eastern half of the United States. Mother would roll the extra watermelons under her bed for later consumption after we had eaten our fill. She loved watermelon so much I can't eat one today without thinking about her or my youngest son. I believed he inherited the love watermelon gene from Mother.

In late August or early September Dad would hitch the tractor to a hand-held plow and we would plow out and pick up our Irish potatoes. There would be bushels and bushels of them.

I always kind of liked that job. You could get dirty as a pig, but there was always the pond or a deep puddle in Salt Creek when you were finished with that chore. Or with the gathering of the ripened hay.

There is no other job on the farm as distasteful as making hay. It is hot, scratchy, itchy and heavy and must be done on the hottest of days. Those days in a hot barn loft are never forgotten.

Then there was the gathering of the ripened pumpkins and field corn later in the fall. The pumpkins were sold at the Morgan Packing Company in Ewing. With no modern elevator to put it in the barn, the corn was shoveled, one heavy scoop at a time, into a vented corn crib for later use as cow, pig, chicken and horse food.

Finally the bounty of summer was picked, dried, canned, frozen, hung from racks, placed in barns or basements and we could take it easy. Sure we could.

About the time all these chores were completed it was time to cut a wood supply for the winter. I liked this part about living on the farm because it kept me outside away from the busy kitchen. Except for catching poison ivy from the trees we cut I truly enjoyed cutting wood.

I am one of those people highly allergic to the juice in poison ivy, so in the fall and winter (when we burned the wood and I got it from that), I always had a case of ivy rashes on me somewhere.

But I loved to cut, load and stack wood. I have finally outgrown that fetish. Give me a nice gas furnace or geothermal heat source any day. For that matter, give me a warm enough climate where a fire is unnecessary to stay warm.

I guess I have gotten soft.

But it sure was a pleasure to walk into the basement of our house to do our daily "shopping."

Dad had built shelving and bins for all the different produce we preserved. There were huge bins of beautiful white Irish potatoes and golden sweet potatoes, apples, squashes, cushaws and pumpkins. There were hundreds of jars filled with all colors of vegetables and fruits. Stone crocks sat right on the cool basement floor and contained dill pickles, pickled beans and corn cut from the cob.

To make pickled green beans you had to start right in the garden again. Pick the beans fresh and string and break them. Place them in a large container with plenty of water and cook over a hot stove until they would pop the bean out with you pressed it with your finger. This didn't take too long actually. Remove from the heat and pour that water off and return the beans to the big pot. In another large pan heat water with large amounts of coarse salt and an equal measure of distilled vinegar, heating until the salt is melted and the water is boiling. Mother always said to use enough coarse salt that the water would support an egg and that would be the right amount for brine. Pour the boiling brine over the beans in their pot and stir well.

You can then fill clean sterile canning jars with the beans and brine. Process the green beans in a pressure canner as directed in the canner's instructions. Remove and place the cooled jars in a cool dark place such as the basement floor or a cellar. You may also place the cooled dilled beans in a large stone crock. If using a crock, weight the beans down with a heavy plat inverted over them and cover the crock securely with cheesecloth to keep the beans clean.

To eat them, some areas call these green beans "dilly beans" for their dill flavor, empty them into a sieve and hold under cold running water to remove some of the salt. Place the washed beans in a hot cast iron skillet into which you have placed some bacon drippings. Cook only until hot through. Serve with cornbread covered with cow butter and drink plenty of water.

You can do the same with sweet corn that has been cut from the cob. Mother liked to mix the corn and the beans together in a crock because of their pretty contrasting colors. The process was the same and this was a much more colorful concoction than plain old beans, but when the corn was added she never cooked them in a skillet. She would always use a pot to heat the bean/corn mix after they were rinsed thoroughly to remove some of the sale. As usual with all her cooking she added a generous dollop of bacon drippings for even more seasoning. However, you do not want to overpower the dill flavor with the drippings so go easy on them.

Mother arranged the jars on the shelves so that alternating colors like yellow corn, green beans, red tomatoes, golden peaches, purple grape juice, green or yellow relishes were attractively displayed.

Each morning she would tell us what she needed brought upstairs to prepare for supper. We would go down with a big bucket and bring up whatever she needed. There was a real treasure trove down in that cold, dark space beneath the house.

By utilizing the resources we raised on our farm there was little need for us to go to a grocery store for anything. Our grocery bill to feed the 10 of us was probably less than $5 per week if that. The only thing I can remember Mother buying was a loaf of white bread to make Dad's sandwiches and cornflakes for Major who must have eaten a train carload of the things in his lifetime. She bought an occasional jar of flavoring from the Watkins peddler to make us a soft drink. Just about everything else we raised ourselves or gleaned from neighboring sources.

We not only had all the produce we needed for the cold season we also had all the farm-raised pork and chickens we could possibly need for the coming cold months.

Around the week of Thanksgiving, if the weather turned cold enough, the hog butchering would begin. All the men in the family, the uncles and some other adults would be advised of the day that the butchering would take place.

Early in the morning, fires would be lit under a 55 gallon barrel and a rope and pulley system would be installed for raising and lowering the hogs into the water to make the hair easier to scrape from the hide. Lots of people now skin the hogs and discard the hides, but there was a lot of fat just under the skin that made useful lard so we always scraped ours. Beside, we all liked the rendered "cracklings" you got when the lard was rendered. Boiling the fats and skins in a large black cast iron kettle over a really hot fire made cracklings.

Someone would stand over the kettle with a long pole, similar to a boat oar, and stir the mixture nearly constantly to keep it from burning. As the fat rose to the top, it would be dipped out with a long handled dipper and poured through a sieve to drain into a lard bucket. After all the fat had been rendered and strained, the remaining meat bits were called cracklings. You could get a handful after they were cooled, sprinkle on a little salt and have a tasty treat. Cooks would mash them up with rolling pins and place the powdered bits in their cornbread.

Once they became too rancid to eat, they could be fed to the farm animals and dogs.

We always butchered at least five huge hogs and preserved their meats in various ways. When I speak the word hog I have to say h-o-g pig because my husband says I drawl it out about a foot long as I say h-a-a-a-a-w-g. I remember one of the first meals from the freshly killed hogs would be a liver and onion supper. That was a real treat and one I still like to serve occasionally. This practice goes back to the stone ages practically, only then the liver and heart would have been eaten raw fresh from the kill.

One of the hogs would be divided among those helping with the butchering chore since several men were required to do the heavy work. That way we did not have to pay any cash out and they, too, would have a nice supply of fresh h-o-g pig meat.

We never tried to save the livers for later. It was prepared and eaten by the helpers and us within a day or two of being processed. If you have never enjoyed a feast of liver and onions you are missing a great treat. Mother always sort of sliced her liver meat about ½ inch thick from down the side, rolled it in flour and fried it kind of slow until it was done. My mother-in-law prepared hers by slicing it thinner and flatwise, rolling it in flour, salt and pepper, and browning quickly in a hot skillet. I believe I like it prepared that way much better than the way Mother fixed it. This is the only food I liked better fixed by someone other than my Mother.

The sausage balls were also excellent. Mother's own recipe was used for the seasoning of the sausage. The sausage was seasoned and rolled into balls, placed in an iron skillet and pushed flat. Then some would be fried and sampled by all to make sure there was enough sage and other seasonings. When it was deemed just right, the entire batch would be made into balls, fried and put into canning jars where it would be covered with the rendered lard and sealed for later use. It would literally keep for years if the jar seal were not broken.

To make her sausage seasoning you will need to do a little experimenting to get just the right mix for yourself. I know she mixed a lot of rubbed sage, coarse salt, black pepper and crushed red pepper in her mixture. Adjust to taste or merely go to the grocery meat section and ask the meat cutter for a package of the house brand seasonings. I have found these are usually pretty nice. Generously sprinkle the seasoning all over the ground meat and mix well. You will have to get your hands right down in the meat to do this properly.

Always do a test patty until you are satisfied you have it right. If you like it better with more sage, add some to the whole batch and remix.

The hog heads were cooked down, picked from the bone and souse made which when it was cold could be sliced and eaten like lunchmeat. I'll never forget the sight of a hog's head sitting in a pot of boiling water with water pouring out both snout holes while it cooked. Every time the lid was lifted to test for doneness there was that nose with the two holes pouring two twin streams into the air. Gross.

The tails, feet, tongue and ears were kept also. Except for the tongue that was cleaned, boiled and sliced, the rest was pickled. In fact, I believe every part of the hog was used but the squeal as the old timers used to say. Nothing was wasted. In much earlier days, even the intestines would be cleaned and used to stuff the sausage in. I can remember seeing that done only one time. Most of the time we canned the sausage or froze it.

The bacon and hams would be sugar cured and hung from wires in the smokehouse to keep any rodents off them. Once the bacons and hams were removed from the carcass, they would be rubbed down with a heavy dose of coarse pickling salt, wrapped in newspapers and tied, then placed inside a clean white case similar to a pillow case, and laid inside the smokehouse to cure for a while. The chunks of meat would be turned over daily so that the salt could penetrate the meat from all angles. After about three weeks, it would be ready to slice. This was known as a salt cure. To sugar cure, the meat would be rubbed with a combination of brown sugar, red pepper, black pepper and salt. The remainder of the process was the same. Others preferred to eat the meat "fresh" rather than cured. If using a salt cure, you need to place the sliced meat in a pan of water, heat to boiling and then rinse to remove some of the salt. Then prepare as usual.

Slicing bacon usually required the butcher to have a very long, very sharp heavy bladed knife. A good butcher could slice those bacon chunks into nearly even strips of meat. It seemed to go better if the meat was very cold, firm but not frozen. You could handle it much easier in that state.

It was wonderful in the wintertime to go into the smokehouse and whack off a slice of the nearly purple cured ham and fry it up with a couple of eggs and eat it with some of Mother's leftover biscuits.

Each spring mother would also order 1,000 baby chicks. At first the young day old chicks would be plopped into a brooder house with a heat lamp until their feathers came in good. Once the chicks had plenty of little yellow feathers and were beginning to show signs of white tail and wing feathers, they could be placed in the regular chicken house, but away from the adult chickens. The chicks

(Mother called them Diddles) needed a place to scatter to safely if a rooster or a brooding hen got too aggressive with them.

After the normal losses and thefts, (one year we lost about 200 to a thief) enough chickens would be slaughtered to feed us for a long time once they were frozen. Others would be offered to neighbors who hadn't a clue as to cleaning them so we usually had to dress them. (That is a misnomer because to "dress" a chicken you first had to "undress" them of their feathers.)

Some of the spring chicken crop would be kept as laying hens. This way we always had a new crop of laying hens coming on. Once we had new layers, the year old hens could then be butchered to use as baking hens or boiled and made into chicken and dumplings. We used all the eggs we wanted and Mother sold the remainder to peddlers and neighbors. Any babies hatched out by these remaining hens would go toward resupplying our dwindling freezer.

Cool fall days were also the time when Mother would decide to make our winter's supply of white hominy. For those who do not know what hominy is, it is corn, but far different corn than one who has never eaten it can understand.

Mother would either plant or purchase or beg from another farm about a bushel or two of large grained white corn. Sometimes she and Dad would drive all the way to Kentucky to find this corn. We would all sit around in the evening and help her shell it from the cob. We had to be careful when shelling that we discarded any bad kernels and we removed as many of the remaining silks as possible.

On hominy making day a fire would be built under our large black kettle somewhere in the back yard and this corn would be placed inside the kettle. Water would be poured over the corn until the pot was full. Once the water started to boil, lye was added. Lye could be bought commercially or sometimes I have seen Mother add sifted wood ashes to the mixture. Once these ashes meet with water, they create lye. Let the pot of corn boil for an hour or more until the corn has swollen enormously.

Pour that water off and wash the corn thoroughly through many cold water baths, rubbing the corn through your hands to remove the black center, until all the lye solution is removed and any chaff or other debris is gone.

Return the corn to the pot and cook until tender. Let it cool and either place it into sterile jars and seal; freeze it; or place it in a stone crock, weighted down with a heavy inverted plate and covered with cheesecloth.

The hominy can be eaten raw with a bit of salt right from the crock or warmed in a pan of grease with salt and pepper added. Merely heat through and serve.

We now would have all kinds of pickles, vegetables, berries and fruits, several kinds of potatoes and all kinds of meats in our food storehouse. We were nearly ready for winter.

By this time in the fall about the only thing left to do to be prepared for the coming cold months was the making of enough lye soap to last until spring. Lye soap was a very caustic soap used not only for washing our clothing it was used in our bath water also. When slivered with a sharp knife into hot washing water for clothes washing, it created a very effective means of whitening our clothing. Your whites would come from the water sparkling white every time.

Kids today know little of how things were done in days gone by. They would probably rebel if told to work in a garden for their supper. My grandson referred to our garden vegetables as "free" food when he was about five and was visiting us from the city. He was thrilled with the idea that we didn't actually have to "pay" for our vegetables as his mom and dad had to do.

But I think we were healthier then even though our life spans are longer now. We knew what chemicals, if any, was on our produce and how all our food was raised and preserved.

Our neighboring Hoosiers were amazed at all the preparations made at our farm. Most of them did not even raise a garden but once they were shown how much the Kentuckians could teach them about self-sufficiency, many of them followed suit and began raising gardens for their families.

I cannot recall if any of them ever went to the extent of trouble we did to make everything, including butchering our own meats, but we surely added something to their knowledge of survival. They, I believe, found out there was a lot more to these strange new neighbors than they had previously believed possible.

Tadpoles, Snakes and Pearls

It was often my job to tend my youngest brother, Major, during the summer time when Mother was busy.

Major was the baby of the family, a preemie, and remained very small until after he reached puberty, then he had a growth spurt, a big one. He remained in the hospital's nursery for several weeks after his birth until he was thought to be able to survive at home. I can remember Mother telling some of her friends that by the time he was a year old he weighed a whopping eight pounds. Surely I misunderstood that statement.

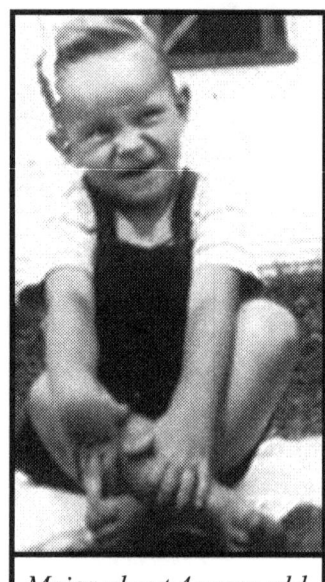

Major about 4 years old.

Up to the time of his arrival I was the imp of the family and my older brothers' laps were my favorite seats. When Dad and Mother brought Major home from the hospital we still lived in Kentucky. The first time I can remember seeing him he was lying in Jimmy's arms, held in his lap where Jim sat on the raised hearth. Well, since that was one seat I considered my own, I pushed Major out of Jimmy's arms onto the floor and climbed into Jim's lap. That little rebellion earned me a good spanking by Jim. It is a wonder I hadn't killed that tiny scrap of humanity he called "The Baby", but he would finally grow on me and I would accept him as one of us.

Once we had moved to Indiana and I was a tad older, if mother was particularly busy doing something I hated to do, she would often tell me to take Major away out of the house and entertain him. I taught him to read adventure stories by reading aloud to him and how to swim, the old fashioned way.

I did that by throwing him into a fairly shallow, by my standards, pool of water in Salt Creek. The creek ran through our town and was about three blocks from our house. "Sink or swim" I would yell as I threw him belly flat into the pool of water. I would wait calmly to see which he did before I pulled him from the water, slapped him on the back until he got his breath, then I would repeat the process. Needless to say he finally learned to swim at a fairly young age.

We read the adventure books of Tom Sawyer, Huckleberry Finn and Treasure Island and many others aloud at home. Then we would head to the creek for the fun of it.

In turbulent times during and after floods Salt Creek could be very dangerous. The rest of the time it ran shallow and clear. You could see to the bottom and see the "oysters" lying there. Major and I called them oysters, but they were really mussels, and we picked buckets full of them from the creek. We were positive as we could be they would contain a pearl when we opened them. The books we read referred to pearls in oysters and these certainly looked like oysters to us so we gathered them. We were going to be RICH, RICH, RICH! We would take the buckets home and dump them onto a table in the backyard.

We would pry them with a knife and strive to open those things to no avail. We quickly found out why their proper name was "Mussels". So we would go away and get involved in another activity for a day or two. A few days later we would remember our oysters and head back to the table. The stench could be smelled from afar. You really didn't want to get too close to the table in the hot weather. The stench was bad enough that not even Roy's hound dog would come close to it.

But we would get close. Really close. We found that if we left them long enough and they died we could open them easily. We checked every shell to see whether we were getting rich. You know, we never did find a pearl. But in our young minds we could see the sheen of pearls, lots of them, and riches galore.

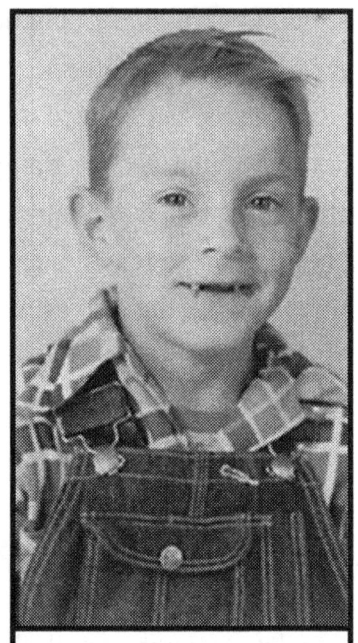

Major missing his front teeth. One of my favorite pictures of him.

We would take Mother a bucket of the shells to use in the house as ashtrays or whatever else she wanted to use them for. There were really pretty inside with the iridescent coloration. Holding her nose she would shoo us back out of the house with our treasure and tell us to clean the mess and ourselves up before we came back into the house.

With a hammer or a big rock we pounded the useless shells into small pieces and threw everything we had collected into the chicken pens. The chickens could make short work of anything we threw at them.

On other days we might hunt for tadpoles in tiny depressions along the edges of the creek. We could spend hours and hours entertaining ourselves trying to catch them in our bare hands and add them to a glass jar full of water.

We would store them carefully in the jar until it slipped out of our hands and then we would have to start all over. When we had collected a bunch of them we would take them to our pond and release them. We had read of eating frog legs and we wanted to grow us plenty of them. But I don't remember ever catching frogs or eating their legs.

Other slow, lazy summer days we would go snake hunting in the creek.

We hunted water snakes and some days we probably found and killed seven or eight by dropping big rocks on them. We were convinced they had to be killed. In our childish minds the harmless little water snakes were cobras and black mambas. Cobras with their spreading hoods and the deadly mambas were other species we read about in books at home. We were convinced everything we killed was life threatening. Poor snakes, harmless but killed by adventurous inquisitive kids.

But that was the way we did things back then. Children were allowed to explore the world around them at their leisure and learn from their mistakes. As long as we were not endangering ourselves, we were allowed to explore or experiment to our heart's content.

Major always loved to play with rocks when he was small. We could spend countless hours meandering along the railroad tracks, selecting pretty rocks that had been dumped along the route to make a roadbed for the trains. None of these stones were from our region of the world so each held a potential interesting background. We carefully stored them in a bucket and brought them home so he would have pretty stones to play with out in the yard.

I was eighteen years old and five foot three when I married. When Major wanted me to wrestle with him I had to get down on my knees so we were the same height. Once I was married a miracle happened. That little kid, Major, had that growth spurt I mentioned when he was about 14. He grew into a strapping six foot, four inch gentle giant. I went on and grew older, but not taller. I still read many books and now try my hand at writing them myself.

Thanks to the tadpoles, snakes and pearls of my childhood I developed an imagination that doesn't want to stop.

Sister Annie

Our sister Anna Ruth was the youngest daughter in our family and was seventh in a string of eight children. She was a short little thing, never growing beyond five foot tall and she was never very large in stature.

When she was born one of her arms was broken and she didn't breathe for quite some time according to the story we were told of her birth. After the doctor placed her in pans of alternating hot and cold water several times, she finally took her first breath, so he splinted her arm. Mother kept that tiny arm splint until we were adults. Annie may still have it.

Annie, young age.

She had light brown naturally straight hair, beautiful gold flecked eyes and didn't look a single thing like any other one of us. We teased her all her life that we found her under a cabbage leaf in the garden and that was why she didn't look like any of us. When she was in her 50's we were attending a family funeral and an older man who knew Mother well told her she looked just like her mother. He ruined all our lifelong teasing with that one remark but it tickled her to death to learn she wasn't adopted or something.

She had the widest, shortest feet I have ever seen. Her feet had tiny narrow heels, extremely high insteps and then extra wide toes. All her life she would have trouble finding shoes to fit her strange feet. A pair of shoes to fit Daisy Duck probably would have fit her quite comfortably. Her feet continually hurt her and she would suffer in the extreme with varicose veins until she had them removed when she was about 40.

The only thing she ever truly wanted to be was a mother. I can remember when she was but three or four years old. She always wore little dresses that barely covered her tiny rear end and showed her panties when she bent over to play. All her dresses, more like jumpers really, could have been cut from one piece of material and contained only the two side seams and the hem. She could wear the same clothes winter and summer, just by adding a blouse or sweater under the jumper.

We never had a lot of money and she never had a lot of toys but she had a vivid imagination. Anna Ruth loved to play house with her dolls and have tea parties, even when she didn't have a doll to play with. If she had one, fine. If not that was fine too because she could pretend she had one. She would place that imaginary doll proudly on a "chair", usually fashioned from a stone and continue with her tea parties, allowing each "doll" to sip from the cup she held before them. All obediently sipped the tea, either real or imagined.

There were squares of stones all over our barn lot and yard where she used those stones to make herself a dollhouse. Those large white stones marked her territory I guess. She would play inside her "house" for hours, dusting the floors with an imaginary broom, humming to herself or telling her "children" stories and holding tea parties. She was never lonesome because she always had her imagination at the ready.

She is still kind of like that.

Sometimes Mother could afford to buy a paper doll for her or sometimes someone else would give her one. She would spend hours pouring through a Sears Roebuck or Penny's catalog, choosing from the catalog's many offerings and cutting out clothing for her paper doll. She would trim the pictures out and leave enough of the other paper around it to make the tabs and paste that dress or coat on her paper doll. Without realizing it she was shopping, one of her favorite pastimes to this very day.

Annie is one of those females who were never hot, nor ever sweated or perspired, as she would say. "I just never get too warm." Fiddlesticks I say. Everyone gets warm sometime, don't they?

When we were very young she would cry to go outside in the winter and play with Sylvia and me. Both Sylvia and I knew that if we had to take her we couldn't stay out long because Annie would nearly freeze to death.

We solved that problem. One day there was about a foot of new snow on the ground and we were determined to go outside and play in it. Annie begged to go with us. We wrapped her up until she could barely move and took her outside. Once outside she immediately said she was cold so we picked her up by her arms and stuck her, feet first, into a snowdrift in the front lawn. There we left her, screaming for help as we ran out of the yard and out into the town. She was so short she couldn't get out of the snowdrift by herself. Finally Mother heard her screams, came out and got her and spanked our bottoms for that trick.

Another time she begged to go sledding with us. Mother made us take her. We kept her out until she was nearly frozen. When we came inside where it was warm Mother had to put Annie's feet in a pan of warm water. She screamed like a banshee as the feeling came back into her frozen toes. She would spend her entire life bundled up with sweaters and such trying to keep warm in the coolest weather.

Annie married young to a man who had been an only child. He wanted lots of children and they presently had five of them two boys and three girls. She was never happier than when she was keeping house for that family, cooking and cleaning. Her childhood fantasies were now reality. She had her own live dolls and spent years dressing them just so in outfits she spent hours washing, starching and ironing.

Even when her children were young and naturally messy you never entered her home that it wasn't spotless. I don't know how she did it because she always worked a full eight hour shift in a factory, came home and rested a bit, cooked either supper or breakfast depending on her job shift, and cared for an ailing husband for 15 years before he died.

After she retired it was normal for her to wake at 3 a.m.—her normal waking time when working the day shift—and immediately start housecleaning. I kept trying to convince her that that was not normal. "There is a cure," I would say. I always hated housework myself and could not understand how someone could wake from a good warm bed at 3 a.m. and start dismantling a home to clean what I would consider an already spotless house.

To me there was no 3 a.m. on my clock. I don't remember ever waking prior to that time nor going to bed after that hour. But she had become used to

Anna Ruth in 2005.

rising early when she worked the day shift so she could clean house and prepare breakfast for her family before she went to work so I guess for her it was natural.

She loves to work in her flowerbeds and it shows. Her home is a showplace in the neighborhood with its flowerbeds outlined with, you guessed it, stones stacked up around them.

She never could get away from piling stones to outline her territory. They were her "nest" I guess. But she finally did get warm one day. I think in the last leap year, during a couple days in the middle of July she finally broke a sweat.

Go for it Annie, enjoy it, live it up.

Sylvia, Helen and Anna at New Year's Eve, early 1980s

The Haystacks

Back in the good old days when I was a kid in the 1950's we made hay the old fashioned way. We didn't have a baler. In fact only one farmer in the neighborhood would eventually have one. We placed our hay in stacks.

Making hay was the hottest, most dreaded job on any farm in those days. It was hard, hot, sticky work and it had to be done on the hottest days of the summer.

First it was cut with a mowing machine that was pulled either behind two horses or a tractor. We did it both ways at one time or another. Once it was cut with that side bar mower it had to be raked by hand with a pitchfork, into rows or small stacks around the field.

Then as the horses or tractor pulled a wagon alongside the rows and stacks, men would use those same pitchforks and throw the hay onto the wagon. It would be stacked up until no more would lie on without beginning to fall from the wagon. Then it was taken to the area in the farmyard around a tall pole implanted in the ground.

There again it would have to be handled. The men with the pitchforks would start forking the hay from the wagon onto the ground around that pole, stacking it higher and higher and wider and wider until a huge mound could be seen.

This process would be repeated until all the hay was harvested and you could barely see the top of the pole sticking up in the middle.

In later years a neighboring farmer would bring his newly purchased hay baler to our farm and hundreds of rectangular bales would be made and tied with that machine. They still had to be loaded on a wagon and brought from the field and loaded into the barn's loft area but this process required fewer handlings than the old way.

Those rectangular bales were a job also. You picked up the quite heavy hay bales by the strings or wires wrapped around the bale to tie them together, bounced the bale on your knee to get leverage, then swung it onto the wagon. At the barn the process was repeated only this time you had to hand it up through the hole in the side of the barn to someone in the barn loft. That person would receive it and hand it behind him to another person who would stack it.

Nowadays that process seems old fashioned. The new bales are huge round bales that no lone man can move. In fact the baler is quite small for the size of the bales of hay. Since one man cannot lift them a tractor with a lift or prong on it is used, now only a single man is required to bring in a big hay crop. He can take the baler into the field, bale the hay, then shift the bales around into rows with the tractor.

Modern ideas have taken the work and also the fun out of hay making.

Fun, you say? Yes, fun.

If you ever saw a haystack you know how appealing that picture was to a kid. It smelled heavenly, was slick and made a natural slide.

We kids would stack up crates or lean an old ladder against the back of the stack and climb to the top. With a shout of glee we would flop down on our backsides and slide to the ground in a big swoosh.

Then we would run to the rear of the stack and repeat the process again and again.

Dad always told us to stay off the haystacks but I never remember him enforcing that rule. I don't think he could have. That haystack was just too appealing. He would have had to miss sleep and keep watch to keep us off it. In fact half the kids in our small town would join in the fun. There was only our farm and one other near the town and our place was one of their favorite places to play.

We could deny to our parents all we wanted to that we had not been on the haystack but there was always enough of it stuck in our hair and clothes, or scratchy places on our arms to give away the truth.

Modern farm kids are missing out on a lot of fun by not having haystacks on their farm. Besides that, a haystack made a dandy sleeping place for the hobos.

Pie Suppers, Quilts and Aprons

When the church I attended as a child needed funds for a major project, the male members always turned to the women to be the fundraisers. If the church needed money to pay the electric or heating bill the men just pitched enough money into a passed hat to pay it. But for the big stuff, the women were in charge. The women came up with many unique and, I think, wonderful ideas to raise money.

I can remember the women making beautiful quilts, each tiny piece hand sewn. Sometimes they would use a sewing machine to put the blocks together, but most women in those days always had quilt squares lying around that they could work on in their spare time. They could do one block, lay it away until they had more time, then pick up another square and continue on. Many different patterns were pieced together in this manner.

When they had enough matching blocks to make a nice size quilt—usually each one was about a foot square—they would attach them to filler pieces until they had a size that would fit a standard bed. There was no king or queen size beds back then that I ever knew of so all the quilts were made for a regular sized bed.

After the blocks were sewn together with the connecting pieces to form the quilt top it would be stretched between two wooden frames and attached with tacks. Cotton batting would be added for weight, warmth and comfort and a bed sheet or soft flannel material added for the backing. Safety pins would be added here and there to hold everything in place until the quilting was finished.

After all that was in place a template would be used to draw a sewing pattern on the quilt's front with a stick of chalk. These designs were sometimes very intricate and pretty.

The women would cook a lunch and spend the day gathered around the stretched quilt to begin the sewing that would turn the top, batting and backing into a beautifully designed quilt. Usually the sign of a "nice" quilt was one that, when turned over on the backside, you could see the patterns of the hand sewing on the front. Most of the time, the women I watched used a fan pattern but I have seen others use a much more intricate design when they quilted.

Every quilt should be as pretty on the back as it is on the front, they said. That was just a standard given. Once the quilting was finished, a pretty binding would be added around the outer edges to make it complete. Often the backing was larger than the quilt's front side so the extra would just be pulled around the edges and sewn down for the finishing touch.

In the mountains of Kentucky a lot of artistic women created what is known as a family story quilt. This would require them using hundreds of small colorful fabric pieces to create pictures of their life, children, farmstead or other pictures on the quilt top. Many of these women quilters could tell you the specific dress or shirt from which each piece of the quilt had been cut. Nearly always, these fabrics would be from clothing that had a specific meaning to the quilter, such as their grandmother's favorite dress or their daughter's bridal dress, etc. Those quilts today remain in cedar chests of the quilter's descendants or in museums where some rightfully belong they tell such a powerful story. I have seen several valued at thousands of dollars.

The younger girls assisted the quilters at the quilting bees by threading the needles and locating the dropped thimbles for the older women or minding the dinner cooking on the stove so that it didn't burn and would be ready by lunch time.

If the quilt blocks had been pieced together on a sewing machine, the quilt was deemed to be not as valuable and the finishing steps were not nearly so complex. Those quilts would be "tied". To tie a quilt to its filler and backing, you merely used a pretty, bright color-contrasted yarn, took big running stitches in rows all over the quilt top, tying the yarn at every stitch, then going back and cutting between the stitches. After the hemming process it was complete. The Hoosiers sometimes called this type of quilt a "comforter", but the Kentuckians just referred to them as a tied quilt.

If there were too many women present to work comfortably around the quilting frame, the extras would be busy cutting out and sewing aprons of all descriptions. There were frilly aprons, clothespin aprons, plain everyday aprons and my favorite, the granny aprons, etc. Every woman in those days had to own several aprons to be always dressed appropriately.

The women got a lot of their material for the aprons by saving the prettily printed feed sacks their chicken or cow feed had come in. Gunnysacking would take the place of these pretty sacks in ensuing years, but when I was a girl nearly everything we wore was made from these pretty printed feed sacks.

Once the feed had been used up, the seam around the empty sack would be removed, the sacks washed, starched and ironed flat. They would be saved for clothing and were often traded by the farm women who needed maybe just one more of a certain print to make that special dress or apron for one of their daughters.

You could use a granny apron in the kitchen or to gather in the eggs, apples or other fruit by holding it up from the bottom to form a basket and placing the eggs or fruit in the apron until you got into the house. Or, you could use it to wipe a tear or a nose of a little one. Or spread your legs and place fresh peas in your lap. You could shell the peas into the apron and throw out the pods. A granny apron was a winner all the way around. And we have all heard about "cutting the apron strings." This meant your child was old enough to act and do and go places on his own. He or she no longer needed to hide behind or be tied to your apron strings.

Usually a granny apron covered most of the front of your dress, had pockets for holding things, a bib and straps which went over your shoulders to form a sort of harness and sashes of the same or contrasting material to tie around your waist. Sometimes the shoulder harness and bib part would have ruffles to make it look like a pinafore. I loved them then and I love them now.

I have a pattern in my files for a granny apron that I have used several times. A much older woman using an opened newspaper made it for me. She used an opened newspaper simply because it was the largest piece of paper she could find to use. There are no instructions written on my pattern. You simply cut out the pieces, match them to where you assume they should go, try it out then do the sewing.

In earlier times everyone wore an apron. They would usually be stored in the kitchen. But a proper woman never answered her door when visitors arrived with her apron on since it might be soiled. First it would have protected her dress, the dress would look fresh so the apron had to be removed prior to admitting or greeting a visitor at the door.

Dad had made Mother a nice peg board containing hooks next to the doorway from the kitchen to the living room so she could hang her apron there and have it available when she returned to the kitchen.

Now these ladies at the quilting bee did not stop with making one or two aprons or quilts. They made several of them. And when they figured they had enough they would hold a rummage sale or a pie supper where they would sell them to the highest bidders.

A pie supper was an absolutely marvelous and fun way to earn money. Every girl and woman would make her favorite pie, put it in a box and decorate it very prettily. Her name would be placed on the box. The man buying her pie got to eat it with her.

If a husband and wife were very jealous of each other, he might bid $25 to $30 for that pie. This was a ton of money for the times but those who knew the couple also knew the man would not let his wife share a pie with any other man so they would "bid him up". This meant they would just push the price higher and higher by bidding against him until they thought they had it high enough he could still afford it, then they would quit bidding and the auctioneer would sell it to the husband.

This happened to my dad once. He paid $25 for a pie mother had baked. No way would he let her eat pie with another man!

There was a much older man who ran a grocery store in our small town who always teased me about my being his girlfriend. He told everyone near and far he was going to bid on my pie. He was a Nazarene but he was going to attend the Baptist pie supper. Little did he know I didn't know a rolling pin from a bowling pin, but I was game to try making a pie.

I decided early in the game to bake a chocolate pie so I would only have to make one crust. I worked and worked on that pie and it was beautiful. I did not know it at the time, but Sylvia had heard this man bragging how he was going to buy my pie so she was prepared.

She helped me decorate my box. I think I was about 10 or 11 years old at the time. The night of the pie supper, sure enough, this old codger bid six or seven dollars for my pie because everyone kept running the price up on him. They remembered what he had told them about how he was going to buy my pie no matter what it cost him.

Well, his was the winning bid and I went over to a table and sat down to eat that pie with him. I cut each of us a big slice and put it on a plate. I wasn't anxious to eat it because I didn't like chocolate pie very well. He took the first big bite, grabbed his throat and covered his mouth with his hand. He ran out the door of the old Masonic lodge hall where we were holding the pie supper, spitting and cursing as he went.

It seems my sister had deliberately exchanged the sugar with salt in the canisters in our kitchen. I had made a pie that was nearly pure salt. This experience served its purpose. He never told anyone I was his girlfriend after that. And I learned a very valuable lesson. Chocolate pie will set up using salt as well as it will using sugar. This fact might prove useful to some.

We would also have a white elephant sale at the pie suppers and during that auction we would sell those beautiful hand-made quilts and aprons. We thought we were making a lot of money, and for the times we probably were, but those quilts would be worth ten times today what we got for them. Especially the hand sewed ones. I'm sure there are plenty of Nazarene families still sleeping under some of those Baptist made quilts.

We also had booths set up for games of chance for every age. One of my best memories is one where Mother dressed as a gypsy woman and told fortunes for a small fee. A sparkling clean upended fish bowl served as her crystal ball. By the time the evening was over, nearly every woman in town with a secret was furious at the gypsy, never realizing it was Mother under all that stage dressing.

All evening Dad had been avoiding telling anyone when he was asked why Mother could not be at the pie supper. "She said she would be here after awhile, she had something she wanted to get done before she came," he would tell them.

Just after the gypsy went away, Mother appeared and the town women told her the awful things the gypsy fortuneteller had told them and had caused them pain. It seems the gypsy had repeated some of their supposed secrets back to them that were not really as secret as they had thought.

To get her exercise Mother walked the three or four blocks to the post office each morning and along the way she would notice who was doing what and with whom they were doing it if they were in plain sight. During the pie supper she relayed back what she had learned on these walks. Some were furious but never connected it with Mother's morning walks to the post office.

She was just trying, in a subtle way, to get them to change their bad habits. I don't know if she succeeded or not, but those women were on their toes for awhile at least. I don't know that any of us ever told these wayward ladies the identity of that gypsy lady

It seems people of today are sort of penny proud and pound foolish. They will spend $100 on a plastic toy for their child but be very frugal when bidding on a pie or something to raise funds for any occasion or good cause. If some of them were only old enough to remember what wonderful times we had as kids in the 1950's, how rich their lives could be today. But every generation has its problems and solutions. I loved our times and solutions best.

Curtain Stretchers

Technological innovations continue to be a boon to the American housewife. Take no-iron curtains for example. Many people today use mini-blinds, shutters, draperies, etc. to cover their windows.

In days of yore every home that had any class at all utilized none of these products. Most could not afford them for one thing, and for another some hadn't been thought of yet. Most of the homes had pull down shades and sheer frilly curtains as window decorations.

Some of the pull down shades were very pretty. A few were made from an almost cloth-like substance with a pretty ruffle at the bottom with a braided cord hanging from the bottom middle to hold to so you could pull it down. Others were made of a kind of paper product, but a very durable one. Others were made of an oiled cloth fabric.

Some people use sheers today under their drapery fabrics. But back when I'm talking about sheers served two purposes. They were light and airy, being made entirely of lace. They gave an illusion of privacy to the people inside the homes when they were closed, yet permitted the outside air to circulate through them freely when the windows were raised and a breeze was stirring. This was in the days before air conditioning was standard in our homes.

Sheers were often beautiful almost diaphanous fabrics, very detailed in design and added a soft, cozy feel to any room. At night the fabric shades behind the sheers would be pulled down to cover windows for privacy when dressing and disrobing.

A good rule of thumb when buying sheers was four times the width of the window if they were to be overlapped in a criss-cross pattern and pulled back with a pretty rope or some other restraint. If they were to hang from the top rod in a pleated fashion, then each sheer should be twice the width of the window to allow for generous pleating.

As beautiful as the sheers were, they took a lot of care even though we never ironed them.

At least once each month every sheer curtain in the house would be taken down and washed gently, usually by hand or if in a washing machine, let run for only a very short time. This was to remove any dust and dirt from the fabric and to prepare the sheers for starching.

Once the sheers were rinsed until no more soapsuds came from them they were dipped into a very thick starch mixture.

When the sheers were removed from the starch mixture they would be taken outside, there to be pinned to the dreaded curtain stretchers.

A curtain stretcher was a very simple yet diabolical invention, probably thought up by a man to "help" his wife. It had a thin slat of wood all the way around its four sides and sat upon a tripod of sorts to keep it from falling and soiling the wet sheers.

Around each side of the wooden slats, about every inch or so, were very sharp tacks sticking out on the drying side. The sheers would be stretched to their utmost and then placed on the pins, first across the top, then down one side, across the bottom and finally up the other side. Many a finger was stuck on those sharp tacks before the sheers were in place. If you listened closely, you also probably could hear a slew of curse words under a woman's breath against the inventor of the contraption.

I don't know, but I am assuming that the curtain stretchers were used so no ironing would be needed on the delicate fabrics once the sheers were removed and ready to be replaced back on the windows. A hot iron might have damaged the fabrics. The stretchers would also tend to keep the cotton fibers from shrinking as they dried. Today nearly every cotton item is pre-shrunk.

At any rate, the tripods holding the white sheers, at that time nearly all were white, would be placed in the sun. There they were left for two or three hours or until the housewife deemed them just as she wanted.

While the sheers were drying, the ladies of the house were busy at other chores, namely washing and polishing the windows and the frames from which the sheers had hung.

A strong solution of water and distilled vinegar would be applied with a washcloth, then newspapers would be used to shine the glass since paper towels were not invented yet or at least not in use in our neighborhood.

The newspapers from several days would be saved for this purpose. They contained no lint as a cloth might have, and left the windows sparkling clean.

At our house these chores were performed at least once a month, winter or summer. It made no difference to our mother. She was a stickler for having a clean house and was a fanatic about her sheers.

Once the window glass was polished, a warm soapy cloth would be used to go all over the wooden window trim. Finally, to complete the chore, a coat of wax or polish would be applied to the wood and buffed to a perfect sheen.

By the time the inside cleaning was done, the sheers would be dry. They would be carefully brought inside, taking pains that none were let down onto the dirty grass or the whole process would have to be done over. I will never forget the sound of the "pings" the curtains made as they were removed from the stretcher. It was almost a musical ping.

Once inside the sheers would be rehung over the now clean windows. The ladies could go to bed that night with the freshness of the outdoors perfuming every room in the house, knowing they had performed a useful function for their families that day.

The smell of the starch and the vinegar on the windowpanes and the lemony smell of the wax on the woodwork were very satisfying aromas.

The Welfare Solution

It seems that more and more people are ending up on the welfare rolls today. When I was a child in the 1950's my mother had a solution to the welfare problem. It didn't involve any branch of the government and required no tax funding. In fact you didn't even have to apply for it. If Mother saw you had a need, you were eligible for her assistance.

Some people were given a small allowance by the county welfare people, but most sort of made do with whatever they had. If mother saw they needed somewhat more than they had she quietly set about providing assistance.

We had a 96-acre farm, which provided us richly with plenty of foodstuffs, pork, chicken, milk, butter and cream, vegetables and potatoes. With a little imagination you could feed a family very well and hardly spend an extra dime in obtaining foodstuffs.

For instance, Mother would have one of us kids catch her a chicken or two from the pens or shoot it through the head with a .22 cal. rifle. If we didn't shoot it she, or one of us girls, would wring its neck by grasping the chicken by its neck, giving it a quick twist with our wrist, throwing it down and letting it flop until it died.

She could take that chicken and pluck it, singe it, dress it and cook it in a big pot of water. After the chicken became so tender it fell from the bones it would be taken from the stove long enough to remove the bones and then replaced in the rich liquid on the stove.

After it came to a rolling boil, she would drop fluffy dumplings into the delicious broth and we would have chicken and dumplings. Add some green vegetables and you had a pretty mouth-watering meal.

Sometimes when she went for her morning walk across town to the post office, she would notice that a particularly needy family's parents were gone again. Usually they were drunk somewhere since that was their major vice.

There were a lot of kids in that family, about ten or more I think they had. Every year or so another tiny scrap of humanity would be added. Anyway they had so many children that not all of them could be raised in their tiny one room log house. Another family nearby raised those extras who would not fit in the one room.

The kids slept in dresser drawers which had been pulled from the chests, in the beds with the parents, on the couch or on the floor. It was not unusual to find a baby in a box on the open oven door.

If she saw that the parents were not at home she would stop and speak with the children who were usually playing listlessly outdoors. They were hungry and she could tell they were by looking at them. If they confirmed her suspicions she would hurry home and start cooking.

Sometimes she made them a huge kettle of chicken and dumplings just like she made for us all the time. Along with those she would send a gallon of ice cold milk and a pound of her freshly churned cow butter and a big pone of cornbread.

Those kids accepted her offerings gladly and would nearly fight to get their share of the contents.

Other times Mother might come home and cook up a big batch of soup beans with some ham cut into them. This would be their dinner along with the milk, cornbread and butter.

I can remember it usually took two or three of us kids to carry that pot and extra stuff across town to their house which stood next to the railroad tracks.

The only thing she would be buying for these meals was the cornbread ingredients. Everything else came from our farm. So for the cost of only a few cents worth of foodstuffs she could feed those hungry kids a wonderful meal.

I don't remember mother ever wanting or expecting thanks from that family for feeding their kids. If she hadn't done what she did on the sly, some of them may actually have starved to death.

This same family moved from across town finally until they lived almost directly across the street on a left diagonal from us. We could see right into their house from our front window because their door was nearly always standing open allowing babies and hound dogs equal access to the home.

When the parents had been drunk long enough or had used up their money, they would return home and beat on those poor kids for any infraction. I can remember once about three or four of them were beaten with a piece of garden hose and locked in the outdoor necessary room for the night. Those kids almost froze to death.

The other people in the town didn't seem to care or were afraid to become involved.

Well, mother couldn't stand to hear them scream and cry. She would call the sheriff's office in Brownstown and a deputy would be sent to arrest the father. The deputies were used to this event because it happened frequently.

The father would go to court, be sentenced to six months at the state penal farm, then return to start it all over again. This went on for years. The welfare system never assisted those kids or the parents. They never once took the kids from the home or found out whether or not they had any food to eat. Mother did more for this family all by herself than a train carload of welfare people ever did for it.

While the father was in the state prison, Mother would make sure this family was on her food donation list every day. She also made sure they had clothes and shoes to wear to school and wood to warm their shack. She was better than General George Patton at organizing the troops to assist this family.

Once to get even with Mother for having him arrested for abusing his children, this man siced his hound dogs on Major as he walked up the street by their house. Those huge dogs mauled my brother pretty badly. He would wear huge bruises on his legs for weeks. The man was truly vicious.

Dad went to the home with his shotgun prepared to shoot the dogs and probably the father if he interfered. The drunk denied he had siced the dogs on our brother and promised Dad he would keep them restrained if Dad didn't shoot them. Dad left him with the warning that he would shoot every one of them if it happened again.

I remember another time mother assisted the town's needy.

The Korean War had ended and all the soldiers came back home, including the three boys, now men, from our family. When they returned, it was to a weakened economy and many of the returning soldiers could not find jobs.

Mother again came up with a solution.

She figured that with so many men needing work and none being available she would turn our farm into a project that would provide the men jobs, her with some money and self-respect for all.

The Old Morgan Packing Company building as it looks today. It has been vacant for many years.

Dad was working for a building contractor so he could not help her much; this project would be her responsibility. She approached the Morgan Packing Company in Ewing and secured a contract with it for all the cabbage and tomatoes she could raise.

We planted five acres of cabbage and about six or seven acres of tomatoes.

I know that doesn't seem like many acres now but in the 1950's we had to depend on backbone for our business. There were no automatic plant setters and tomato pickers then. Nor were there any migrant workers in our area at that time. We had to rely strictly on the manpower available in the little town.

Each plant we planted had to be put into the ground by hand. Each cabbage hoed and cut by hand. Every tomato picked by hand. All the crops were labor intensive; that is why she chose these vegetables.

To prepare the plants for setting in the ground Mother would sit at the end of the row in front of a mud puddle she had made, dipping a handful of plants into the mud and placing each handful on the top of a tomato "mater" plant lid. She thought this would provide extra moisture for the roots so they could take hold better. Morgans would provide beautiful plants for her and she wanted to preserve as many of the plants as she possibly could.

One of us girls would carry that tray of muddy plants alongside each row and hand them, one plant at a time, to the men. They would take a short hoe, strike it into the ground, pull back on it to make a hole and stick in a plant. As they walked to the next space, they would tamp the plant with the toe of their shoe to tighten the dirt to the roots. The length of each of the men's stride determined how far apart each plant would be set.

In order to get the plants in the ground and tended and harvested Mother would open the fields to anyone in town, man or woman, who wanted to work.

I think she only paid about ten cents per bushel of tomatoes picked. You would take a chit with your name on it and place it in your basket of tomatoes. The full baskets would be placed in an empty row down the length of the field. Two rows would be left vacant as we planted to make room for a truck to drive through and pick the produce up. As the tomato boxes were picked up, the chits were removed and kept by Mother so she would know how many bushel each person picked.

Men would set the filled baskets up on the trucks to another guy who would stack them until the truck was full. Then it would be delivered to Morgans, sold and the truck would return for another load. Let me tell you, six or seven acres of tomatoes will fill a lot of baskets. Sometimes if Morgans was really busy, you could see wagon loads or truck loads or produce backed way up into the town of Ewing waiting to unload.

I cannot recall how much she paid for each cabbage cut. I think, though, she paid those on an hourly wage.

The work was hard, but honest and many people came to the fields to work. This went on for three or four years until most of the adult men had found other jobs and we were sick and tired of raising tomatoes and cabbage so she quit raising produce for the market.

These were just some of the ways she had for dealing with poverty and need. Most men didn't want or like to be seen as failures by their family. By assisting Mother in raising these crops they could keep their dignity and make some money and she could earn some money for our family.

And the family of the drunk she helped?

The last time I saw him he told me he wanted to thank Mother for her assistance to his family. He said he had shed his addiction to alcohol, joined a church and had become a Christian man.

I accepted his thanks for Mother, but advised him she had been dead for a couple of years. I truly believe he was remorseful and I just as truly believe Mother heard his apology and praise for her.

Sylvia's Drowning

My older sister Sylvia was always something special and different. In high school she wore pumps, nylon hose and a girdle to school every day, and she has never changed her habits in all these years. She wears similar clothing today. I have seen her go to exercise class wearing slacks, but you can bet underneath them was her girdle. But back when she was in high school in the 1950's it was almost unheard of for any student to wear nylons and pumps to school.

Occasionally she would wear the brown and white or black and white saddle shoes with rolled down bobby socks, but not very often. She never felt "dressed" in that type of clothing and footwear.

In summer she would wear shorts and tops much like the rest of us and sometimes bare toes could be seen peeking forward, but that would have been rare.

Young Sylvia

She caused a town scandal when she bought the first two-piece swimsuit ever seen worn in the little town where we lived. By today's standards that suit would look like a granny dress. It left her midriff bare and showed a lot of slender shapely leg, but it did not by any means show her butt cheeks, and it completely covered her bosom. It really was very tasteful.

She had earned the money to buy it by shucking sweet corn for a neighboring farmer and ordered the suit from a catalog. It was made of a green and white flowered spandex-like material and really looked quite nice on her. She would shock old Miz Smith, an 80 plus year old woman that lived across the street from us, each time she put it on and walked out into the yard.

Not long after she bought the suit she and a friend, along with yours truly, decided to go for a swim in Salt Creek, which ran near our house. There was a deep hole of water where you could swim or fish. We walked there and discovered that due to a heavy rain the night before the creek was swollen almost out of its banks and was running swift and muddy.

I had been afraid of water all my life and would not go into the water. Sylvia and her friend dove off the bank and immediately disappeared, swept around a bend and across to the other side. I thought they had drowned. I hollered for them but they could not hear me over the roar of the water.

I started running for home screaming for help as loudly as I could. I could hear what sounded like girls screaming across the creek. Petrified for her I just cried harder and ran faster.

Reaching home I roused mother who ran all the half-mile to the creek hollering like a banshee and further alerting the town to a possible drowning. She was crying and praying and running. I don't remember Mother ever running very often or ever that fast. She was sort of heavyset and it was hard for her to run, but she certainly ran that day.

Everyone in town who heard the screaming and saw the others running toward the creek came to help. I relayed all I knew about what had happened and what I had heard and I told all and sundry that both the girls had probably drowned. Then I cried even harder.

But the story of her demise was greatly exaggerated. She and her friend had not drowned. A short distance from where the girls entered the water there was a group of local boys swimming, including Roy, an older brother of ours.

The boys, seeing the two girls being swept around the bend in the creek, and seeing me running and hearing me screaming thought it would be funny to cry out like girls and make me think they had drowned. They succeeded admirably. When they realized that I believed them, they then started yelling trying to slow me down. But with my loud crying and screaming for help I could not hear them, so I ran on to alert the town.

Soon it appeared the entire town was ready to start launching rowboats to look for the girls. But before they could launch one the girls returned.

About a half-hour after I had spread the alert, both girls came strolling through the streets of town, unaware everyone was looking for them.

When they were swept around the bend and to the other side of the creek they had to leave the water on that side, walk a fair distance along the railroad tracks back to town, then return to their homes.

I will never forget Miz Smith crying out, "Lordy, Lordy, there Sylvia is. She's not drowned at all. Wouldn't it have been awful if she had drowned in that new suit."

I never understood whether she thought it would have been a waste of a good swimsuit or scandalous to arrive at the pearly gates in that two piece swim suit.

As for the boys who caused the confusion to begin with, they were severely disciplined by their parents and they promised never to do that again.

It's a good thing Sylvia didn't drown because she has added much to our family structure over her entire life span. She took the place of Mother in the kitchen after her death, collecting all Mother's recipes, keeping the family cohesively attached to each other.

She has two sons. Her oldest son and my oldest son share a birthday, but hers is one year older than mine. A devout churchgoer just like Mother, she spends a good deal of her time doing things for her church family.

Sylvia spent many years living in Pontiac, Michigan where she and her husband returned to after their stints in the Air Force. Both are veterans. They moved to Western Kentucky just south of Evansville after her husband, Jerry Ziegler, retired from Bell Telephone where he had worked for many years.

Except for a couple of years working in Pontiac, she has been a stay at home wife, where we tell her she "never did work or hold a job." She quickly tells anyone who says that phrase in her hearing, that she busted her butt working in her home and taking care of her family all these years. "That is a big job," she reminds us.

I have to agree with her. Maintaining a happy home and family is a wonderfully rewarding 'job."

House Building

Building your own home with the sweat of your own brow and the brawn of your own back with only the most basic carpentry skills is a formidable, but very rewarding task. Add to that the fact you have only a hand-drawn outline of what the floor plan will look like doesn't help a whole lot either. But we did it and had a good time doing it. We built not only four homes for our own family, we helped my husband's brother build two and a cousin one. We assisted several others in remodeling jobs becoming very adept at our carpentry skills.

That first home took us a while to complete.

We bought almost two acres from one of my husband's aunts for the grand sum of $200 and we had to pay on that amount for over a year. We didn't make a lot of money, but we were very frugal with what we did earn. While paying off the debt his aunt allowed us to go ahead and start clearing the brush and green briars from the property.

We worked long hours after work and on weekends. The two boys were just babies at the time so one of the first things we built was a sandbox for them to play in with their big Tonka trucks. They loved those big yellow, nearly indestructible trucks and bulldozers and would entertain themselves for hours.

We found an old beat up refrigerator to keep their milk and a little food in so we wouldn't have to waste time by going back to our rented home and fixing meals. The purchase of that refrigerator would give us quite a scare a bit later in our house building efforts.

One day we were working and the boys were playing together peacefully. Then we noticed Douglas was missing. We started looking and yelling for him. He would answer but very faintly. We searched the attic, the basement and all around the house. We looked in the bathroom, bedrooms, kitchen cabinets, but no Doug was found. At the end, Mickey went by the refrigerator and for some reason opened the door and out fell Douglas into his arms, nearly asphyxiated. It was an older style and the door locked when he climbed inside to hide from Lonnie.

Another day the boys were playing in the sandbox and we are busy doing jobs around the house site, not paying a whole lot of attention to them. Then we heard the youngest one scream. I grabbed him up and it became very obvious the boys had been in a sand slinging fight and the baby got the worst of it. Douglas had sand in his eyes, nose and ears and it was all around his mouth. I rinsed him off in a rain barrel the best I could and spanked the older boy. For a week when his bowels moved, there was sand in his diaper so he had also swallowed a bunch of sand. It's a wonder it didn't kill him. But they were tough little boys.

Wages were very skimpy in the early 1960s, but we managed to save a small amount from nearly every paycheck to apply to our house building account. When we had at least $50 saved up we would pack up the boys, a pound of bologna and a loaf of bread and head out to the lumberyard. The ones with the most affordable materials were about 60 miles away from where we lived. If we got hungry along the way we could always stop and fix us a sandwich.

The rental house we had lived in for about two years had burned one day while we were going into town for a job interview for me.

We used some of the fire insurance money to purchase an older pickup truck to use in our project and we got a lot of mileage out of that investment.

On lumber buying days the four of us would pile in our old truck and head out for a day's fun adventure. Most of the lumberyards we patronized would let us sort and load the truck ourselves and that is what we did so we could get the very best grade of lumber we could afford.

When we left the yard loaded with lumber, that old truck's back end would nearly be dragging the ground and we had to drive really slowly on the way home. Some of the lumber would be longer than the truck's bed and would bounce up and down as we drove down the road. I felt like an Okie from Muskogee in that old truck with all the stuff bouncing around in the back. It is amazing to look back now at today's prices and realize just how much lumber we could get for that $50. At our building site we would carefully sort and stack our latest batch of material and cover it with tarps to keep it dry.

Mickey's Grandma Lizzie paid to have the local dozer contractor come in and dig us a basement. We laid the blocks, mixing all the mortar by hand. We ordered cement from a mixing plant when we poured the floor. Finally we were ready to start nailing some of that lumber on the top part of the house. Since all my brothers and my dad were carpenters, electricians or roofers we had ready made experts to advise and occasionally assist us, but most of the work we did ourselves. If we didn't know how to do something I would buy a book or find one in the local library to show us how. In later years both Dad and my brother, Glenn, paid my husband the highest compliment they could give. "You know as much now as we do about building. You don't need us anymore."

Finally, we had the house under roof. One of our uncles was a finish and trim contractor for a large corporation. Hardwood flooring had been installed in a home he was trimming for someone else. The flooring got wet and buckled and it all had to be removed. My husband did that, hauled the wood home and removed all the nails. We used that wood for our flooring and it turned out beautifully. We had to do a lot of sanding, varnishing and buffing, but it was really pretty, just hard to keep dusted. We would later cover it with carpet in a later remodeling project.

We decided to move into our basement and save the rent we had been paying and finish the house while we lived below. It was dry and warm and quite cozy. We lived in the basement about a year and a half before disaster struck. One cold, rainy February night we went to bed after a nice Valentine's dinner. It had been raining steadily for several days but the place was dry and warm. I woke in the middle of the night hearing what sounded like a rifle firing inside the basement. It was the back wall caving in. The steep hillside behind the house, disturbed by our dozing efforts, slipped down and came right through the house. We were petrified and very lucky.

My husband jumped out of bed when he realized what was happening and there was about a foot of water and mud in the basement and more coming in all the time. I had reached under my side of the bed and placed my glasses there before I went to sleep. Without them I am blind.

He started searching for the boys in the dark, being too afraid to try to turn on lights afraid of being electrocuted. He finally found the oldest boy's hand but yelled that he was dead. I said, "Pull him out anyway." He did and handed him off to me then started trying to locate the baby. As soon as he pulled Lonnie from under the wreckage, his bed disintegrated. We later found a piece of wood about 1 foot long. That was all that was left of his bed. It had been under a huge slab of concrete blocks and mud. We got him out just in time.

Then he said he couldn't find the baby. Doug had crawled to the opposite end of the bed from that which we had placed him at bed time but he finally grabbed him. By that time we were nearly in shock, cold and in our night clothes.

We ran outside to that same old truck. My husband had on only a pair of long johns, no shoes or anything else. He had to lead me because I was blind without my glasses, in the dark and pouring rain.

He tried to start the truck and flooded it. The boys were still asleep, one in my arms, the other in the truck seat. Mickey decided to run to his Grandma's and borrow her car and take us down there. She lived about one half mile away and he ran every step of the way in his bare feet, borrowed her car keys, then also flooded her car he was so nervous.

He ran back to our house and grabbed the biggest kid, I took the baby, and he led me as he held to me with one hand. We ran back through that rain again. The boys didn't wake up until we were almost inside Grandma's door. She took the baby from my arms and I promptly fainted.

The next morning Mickey went back to our basement and felt around in the mud until he found my eyeglasses. We lived with my parents about a week until we found another rental house and started repairing our home.

About three years after we started building our house, it was finally finished and was beautiful. We lived in it for a few years and then decided it wasn't large enough, the boys needed their own room, so we started an addition and swapped ends with our house. What had been the kitchen became a large bedroom, the living room became a bedroom and one of the bedrooms became the new kitchen area. We added a dining room, huge living room and front porch.

Finally we each had a bedroom. The boys had spent their entire lives sleeping in the same room in separate beds. We assumed they would be overjoyed to have their own rooms. We were wrong. They would go to bed in separate rooms each night and before morning one would go the other's room and sleep on the floor by the bed. We finally just left them to sleep in whichever bed they wanted to sleep in.

Then I found a forty-acre farm for sale about nine miles away and we bought the farm, sold that house and started building another. We just recently completed revamping and swapping ends with this house also. I can't believe we have totally rearranged the rooms in two houses in our lifetime, but we did.

I was working at the local job corps center when we were building that first house. Since I was a good typist I was assigned to work for the center's director. Being in that office meant that I was sort of an upper crust employee according to the standards in the public affairs office.

As part of their work, they send the upper echelon employees a questionnaire so they could profile each of us in the company's newsletter.

One of their questions was, "What do you do for a community project?"

I answered, "What are you talking about. I am the community project." After I had been with the company for a while I didn't have to explain further, as first one disaster after another befell us.

My husband and our oldest son each broke an arm, not once each, but twice. My husband, who appeared to be a young, strong healthy man had to have his superior vena cava replaced. For those who do not know what this is, it is the largest vein in the human body and brings the blood back to the heart from the head and arms. He lived through the experimental surgery and did well. I also had several major health setbacks while working at the center.

It was fun working there and my family became the subject of many a funny incident, one of which made the wire services.

My husband is a pushover for animals. He once brought me a young skunk he found beside its mama that had been run over by a car and killed. He had carefully wrapped the baby skunk in his new tee-shirt and tied it to his windshield wiper and brought it home. When he got there the skunk was spraying like crazy. Mickey wanted me to hold the skunk out the window by its tail and we would take it to the vet to have it descented and make a pet of it. I made him release the skunk and bury his clothes in the garden.

To get into the Job Corps Center you had to stop at a guard shack at the entrance and show your picture identification card. Well, with my car smelling like a skunk, the guards would just see me coming, pinch their noses and wave me on through.

Public Affairs finally asked me if I had run over the skunk and I told them the story. They printed it in the newsletter and it made the wire service.

For a little while we were famous.

Ain't Love Grand

Love, aaah, ain't it grand. That is, the old fashioned kind of love we saw between our parents, kinfolk and later on down the line, between our siblings and their mates.

Our parents enjoyed 54 wonderful years together. Most of the siblings have now been married 30-50 plus years. The same goes for our cousins. When we fall in love we land with a thump and we stay there. Two brothers and one sister lost their mates to cancer or heart disease after about 30 years of matrimony. Those are the three exceptions to our rule.

Mother & Dad, 50 year picture.

But staying in love does not happen by accident. You have to work at it. All it really boils down to is a little give and take. He gives a little and you take a little. No, folks I am kidding. That is like when I was dating my future husband he was always giving me odds, "heads, I win; tails, you lose." It took me a while to figure that one out but I finally smartened up.

Our parents married after their third date. Sylvia and I decided after our first date with certain fellas that they would one day become our husbands and they did. But between the brothers and the other sister, falling in love was almost as quick. We were not known for shilly-shallying around when it came to choosing our mates or making up our minds. Find them, woo them and wed them. After that, it is too late. They couldn't get away or change their minds. Each one of us feels we got the best mate.

Mother and Dad had a rough way to go to keep the spark alive. With eight children underfoot every day, all day, it became a problem to find time to spend with just the two of them. They often went for tractor rides to the "back forty" just to get away from us. We had 96 acres on the farm so there was always a crop that needed to be looked after or so they would tell us. Now we kids were pretty smart people. We did not need a roadmap drawn for us to know they needed some time away from us.

When mother was cooking and Dad was home, she had trouble maneuvering around in the kitchen. He would sit at the table and talk to her as she cooked. Every time she went by him to get something out of the fridge he would grab her and pull her onto his lap and kiss her resoundingly. Mother would playfully swat him on the shoulder and remind him if he kept that up his dinner would be delayed. But he didn't care and he didn't stop. Open signs of affection between them were an everyday happening at our house.

Sometimes when several girls had gotten off the school bus to spend the night with us they would be amazed at just how many kisses got passed around before bedtime. "Are they always this way," they might ask. I believe the activity was kind of catching. All of us kids do the same thing with our mates. We are not afraid to show affection. In fact, I find it utterly strange to be around a couple that doesn't kiss or cuddle when one is leaving and they are in the company of others. I have never thought a thing about it. My husband and I just kiss. Sometimes I stay puckered up and tell him, "I need one more, my lips won't unpucker until you do and they will have to stay this way all day." He may think I am nuts but he always obliges me.

Something as simple as a spontaneous hug or a kiss on the neck (or the top of my husband's bald head in our case) goes a long way toward restoring harmony in a household after a spat. You can't stay mad at someone you are kissing and hugging. I guarantee that.

Mother had several tricks up her sleeve for pleasing her man. She rose very early every morning to fix Dad and all the kids a variety of hot foods to eat before they started their day. I cannot remember ever rising and not finding a hot breakfast waiting for me once I was dressed.

By noon, Mother would be really tired. She had already been up and about the house and barn doing chores for 8 hours usually and had done a ton of work and taken her walk to the post office.

There was a radio show called "Ma Perkins" that she loved to listen to. It came on the radio just about noontime. She would have already fixed herself a hot lunch; she never ate cold sandwiches like most of us do today. She would take her lunch into the living room and place it on the coffee table and tune in Ma Perkins.

She would listen to the program while she ate, then it was time for an hour's nap. Lying down on the couch she would very soon be snoring softly. You could have set your clock by her schedule. When she awoke from her nap she was refreshed and ready to complete her busy day. She ran a bath and soaked in the warm, scented water until it started to cool then would step out, powder and paint herself very lightly, and put on a fresh housedress, hose and heels. She never wore anything other than heels until she was much, much older or was working in her garden. She kept her hair tidy with regular permanents and visits to the beauty parlor and never had need of hair color. Her hair remained warmly brown to her dying day.

By that time she was as fresh and prepared as she could be to welcome her good-looking man home from the trenches. Then it was time to fix supper for all of us. It was always, without fail, ready to place on the table as soon as Dad got home and had taken his bath.

When she saw him pull into our driveway Mother would turn the taps on in the tub for his bath. By the time he walked inside his bath water was ready. Clean clothes would be laid out for him on a chest in the bathroom. She would stay to wash his hair and his back, then leave him to complete his bath and dress himself. I often wondered how he managed to do that much for himself. I never saw him when he could go to his chest of drawers and find clean underwear for himself. Mother always did that chore.

When he stepped from the bathroom, he was groomed for the evening and coming night and ready for work in the morning. Mother would check his feet to see if they needed rubbing with lotion or his athlete's foot problem needed her attention. He worked as a carpenter, often in damp spaces, and this contributed to his foot problems so she kept a close eye on them.

Once mother was satisfied she had done as much as she could to ensure his comfort and well being, she walked with him to the kitchen table and set his food before him. She would not have to call us to supper. When we saw Dad pull into the driveway we stopped what we were doing and made our way to the house. We knew it was time for supper. As soon as all of us were gathered around the table we started eating and talking about our day or about what we had learned in school. Dad would tell us which project he had been assigned to work on that day and how his work was progressing. Mother would read aloud any letters we had received that day. All the news of the entire clan would be shared.

It was around that kitchen table at supper time that we learned our brother Palmer, then stationed in Alaska during the Korean War, had been called upon to shoot a man who was trying to blow up the ammunition dump. Mother's hand was shaking as she read, but she shared that news with us.

When the song, "Come Home, Come Home, it's Supper Time," was released I would think of my family every time it was played.

I don't know of another man who was ever pampered as much as my Dad, unless it was my brother-in-law Jerry, or my five big, brawny, equally good looking as Dad, brothers.

These men were not dumb. They saw the service Dad received and made sure they married women who would do the same for them.

We women tend to sort our men's clothes after we pick them up from where they have been dropped on the floor, wash them, turn them right side out and fold them before placing them back in their assigned drawers. If mending is needed that is done before being returned to the drawers. In my case, if any of this ever varied, my husband would be totally lost. But in my case, if something needs mending it either gets hidden or thrown away. I do very little mending and this drives him absolutely crazy. But he can find his sock and his underwear drawers at least. I'm not too sure I can say that about my brother-in-law. I have never seen Jerry fix a sandwich or pour a glass of milk for himself. In fact, I wonder if I have ever seen him open the refrigerator door. I'll have to think about that a while. Sylvia totally spoils him rotten and he loves every minute of it.

Sib & Jerry, latest picture.

Sister Annie asked Jerry once if he would recognize a refrigerator when he saw one and he assured her he knew what they looked like. "Have you ever looked inside one," she asked. Jerry had to admit he had peeked in a time or two. "Do you know what they are used for," she further questioned.

How many of my brothers are like Dad? Each and every one of them, however the youngest of the family does tend to assist his wife about as much as she helps him. Major even rises first in the morning and makes her a nice "cuppa". She is from England and must have her cup of tea or now, coffee, before she leaves her warm bed. We have changed her drinking habits a bit I guess.

Once when Dad's sister, our Aunt Margie, was visiting with me I took her on a tour of our beautiful wooded county. We talked ourselves nearly to death that day then came home and I fixed us a nice lunch. Aunt Margie asked me if there was a lot of love in our family. I assured her there had been. "I just wondered," she said. "Your folks were always so crazy about each other I didn't know if they had any love left over for you children."

Now you understand the guy who wrote the lyrics to the song, "I Want a Girl, Just Like the Girl, Who Married Dear Old Dad." The writer of that song wanted someone who would wait on his every need.

So when someone says to you, "Ain't love grand," you can either agree with them if you are like us, or, you can admit you really do not know. Here's hoping everyone can find the happiness we have.

I wrote the following song/poem after I saw my brother Jim and his new wife Becky smooching in the restaurant where they had met each other. Becky has been my sister-in-law twice. First she was married to my husband's brother, Richard, who died of cancer. A year later Jim's wife, Barbara, also died of cancer and I introduced the two of them and the rest is history.

Lolly-Gagging

I saw grandpa kissing grandma--in the kitchen the other night.
Both had lips puckered up, and their eyes were shut real tight.
What are you doing, Grandpa? --Why does she look like that?
Son, he says, when dealing with women--this is how you act.
Having a wife is mighty nice—when everything goes your way.
But cross her or boss her—there's only one way to atone.
If you want your way, at the end of day—take this advice.
Be real nice, all honey and spice—and know the words of this song.

> CHORUS:
> *You got to pitch some woo, and bill and coo*
> *Then do a lotta lolly gagging.*
> *After that you got it made*
> *And it sure cuts down on the nagging.*

Well, what he said had the ring of truth, and I thought I'd try it out.
I watched ma and pa, and brothers Jim and Glenn
Their wives gave in, with a silly grin—and I gave a shout,
Grandpa was right, and that's a fact—cause they were all lolly gagging.
If it works for them and Uncle Tim--will it work on the birds and bees?
Lo and behold, as I noticed them--and the dogs and cats and such.
Eyes rolled around and tails started wagging--and I was sure dumb struck
After dashing around, in a mad rush--they all went to lolly gagging.

> CHORUS
> *I'll remember this, when my time comes--to take a woman to wife*
> *This will be my secret weapon--all the days of my life.*
> *When I want to play cards, or run my dogs--or just stay out all night.*
> *I'll grab my wife, and hold on tight--and do a lotta lolly gagging.*

©*February 27, 2000*
Written by: Helen C. Ayers

Learning to Drive

Learning to drive never seemed to me to be too difficult. You jump into a vehicle, turn the key, engage the gears and go. Sometimes, if no one else has done it, you need to add a little fuel. If you wait long enough another someone will usually check the fluid levels and the air in the tires. Not everyone needs to do these chores. I learned to drive at a very young age, beginning when I was about 11 years old on a farm tractor and flatbed truck. It was not so easy for other members of my family however.

It is amazing to me how some women just cannot learn to drive. Is it because they do not want to learn or do some women have a mental block about this? I'm not sure. I personally never had trouble learning, but I was forever lost and still am. While other members of my family are like homing pigeons, I stay perpetually lost. If I am reading a map while my husband drives, I'll turn the map north, south, east or west depending upon which direction we are assumed to be driving. He once saw me holding the map upside down and asked me what I was doing. "Reading the map, silly. We are going south, so we are going down. This way I know where I am." Some people just don't know anything.

In the early days of their marriage Dad tried to teach Mother to drive. She just never quite got the hang of it. She finally quit trying to learn when she nearly ran over him as he was outside cranking the car for her. It started and she already had it in gear. The car jumped at him as he jumped to the side. Mother shut the thing back off, exited the car and never got behind the wheel again.

It became a job for the newest licensed driver in our family to drive Mother to town on Saturday so she could pay her bills. All her appliances were bought "on time" and every week she was required to pay so much until she had the bills paid. Every appliance store in those days offered their products for $1 down and $1 week. Mother took them up on lots of appliances for our home. Mother generally paid her honest debts with her "milk and butter" money. This money was earned by her work alone. She was able to raise enough extra money to more or less furnish our home by selling the extra milk, butter and eggs she sold from the farm to the neighbors. She generally earned enough to pay her debts off well in advance of the due dates because she made payments a little over the $1 week rate.

You could not just drive mother from business to business, drop her off, and wait. It didn't work that way. You drove her to town, found a parking place that was centrally located and that evening returned home with her. She would walk in and out of every store in town it seemed like to buy ten cents worth of something here and a dollar's worth there. I am one who hates to shop. Maybe having to drive Mother for two years until the next kid got her license is the reason for that. Anyway it was a job each one of gladly relinquished when the next one came of age to drive.

Every merchant in Seymour and Brownstown knew Mother by sight and some by name, especially the people at the Murphy's five and dime in Seymour. She could spend hours inside Murphy's. Sometimes she would buy something, sometimes not. But usually she would buy at least a dollar's worth of sugar wafer cookies. I still love those things. They came in chocolate, strawberry and vanilla flavors. She usually got some of all three flavors. Or at Christmas time it was hard candy or chocolate haystacks. For one dollar you could buy a lot of goodies.

A sister-in-law, Juanita, also never learned to drive. She was married to our older brother, Glenn. She, too, would have several mishaps behind the wheel. Another sister-in-law, Bridget, or Bea as she would come to be called was really a wicked learner. But she was handicapped by having to learn to drive on the busy streets and interstates in New Jersey.

I visited with brother Palmer and Bridget when I was 14 years old. I stayed two weeks with them and didn't breathe an easy breath whenever I was in the car with Bea and she was behind the wheel. It was always an experience. She would say to me as she drove down an interstate highway at 60 miles per hour, "Helen, you will never learn to drive unless you can pick your nose at the same time. Just look around you, every driver is picking his nose." You know, I believe she was right. She didn't like it that I had already been driving for three years, but no law officer ever questioned me when I had to drive to Brownstown or Seymour on farm business.

The night before Bea was to get her driver's license we went for a spin with her to let her get in some practice time. While driving sedately down a residential street she came upon a barricade. The road was closed ahead so she was forced to make a very tight turnaround in the middle of the street. She was doing a pretty good job of things until she had to back up a little bit. When she made that maneuver, she backed over a fire hydrant, breaking it off. The force of the water very nearly lifted the car with all its occupants off the ground. She quickly sped away and she would deny ever running over the thing. Bea is a hotheaded Italian. I did not want to argue with her too much but I sure was glad to get out of that car. I have seen that same scene many times since in cartoons. I honestly think someone saw her back over that hydrant and she became the model for the cartoons.

When my grandson decided he wanted to learn to drive my son gave up the reins. "Mom will teach you," he said and shipped him to me from Spain where they were living at that time. I spent an entire summer getting him a learner's permit and trying to teach him to drive. By the end of that time I was a haggard wreck. It took me two summers and two permits before I could whip him into shape. I did learn something though; he stays as nearly lost as I am so we are definitely genetically connected.

I am including with this story a copy of the diploma I gave Victor when he was finally able to get that all-important driver's license. Look out world, here comes another one of us. Someone get ready to save the pieces. Maybe Rand McNally will send him a road atlas.

Grandma's Redneck School of Driving

This certificate certifies that
VICTOR SAMUEL AYERS

Has completed a comprehensive study of the American automobile. He is now authorized to: carry his shotgun in the rear window of his pickup; drive with one hand and flip the bird with the other; drive with one hand and pick his nose with the other; rearrange his package with one hand and drive with the other; scream at other drivers; cuss other drivers; cut corners; stop and look at foliage while traffic backs up behind him; vary his speed up and down at his pleasure; and various other unnamed privileges. He also was taught to check his fluid levels, air pressure; repair minor dings and dents and how to replace the electric antenna.

For these accomplishments I have set my hand and seal and declare that he may drive any vehicle made by man. Dated this 26th day of July 2000.

Pix of Mickey handing Victor a set of keys for the pickup truck we bought him to use in College.

Grandparent Pictures

I don't mean to bore you by bragging on my grandchildren, but they, like yours are very special.

Our grandson, Victor, has spent more time visiting with us so I had more pictures of him. His sister, Mercedes, who is five years younger than Victor still has a special place in our hearts and we do not mean to slight her, it is just we have fewer pictures of her than we did of her brother.

So here are a few family pictures I just could not fit into any of the foregoing stories.

Mickey and Victor when Victor was young. They always had a good time playing together. Here is Victor's reaction to sitting on a motorcycle with his grandpa.

This is our beautiful granddaughter, Mercedes with a palomino horse a friend loaned her to ride during one of her visits with us. Notice that she is taller than the horse, unlike her grandma whose head is only stirrup high.

Victor appears to be assessing whether it would be worth keeping his sister, Mercedes in this picture. I'm glad he decided she was a keeper.

Douglas was assisting his Dad at the drilling site one day and got his picture taken.

Lonnie and his son, Victor, were caught in a very moody picture. I love how relaxed they seem.

Those Lying Hound Dogs

If there is one thing in life I have learned to mistrust it is lying hound dogs. Usually you can't believe a word a dog says.

Now most people don't believe that dogs can talk in the first place so they probably won't read any further than the first paragraph of this story. But I know better. They not only can speak English (or German or Russian as the case may be) but they can tell whoppers as well.

My family has had hound dogs of one sort or another all my life. It started out with a dog named Rover that was owned by my brother Roy when I was just a kid. He could tell some pretty tall tales.

Living in a small community as we did, there were a lot of dogs named Rover. They mostly came from the same litter of pups and were identical in looks. You hollered, "Here Rover" when it was time to feed and nearly every dog in town would come to eat supper. Now most of those dogs loved to come to our house for a meal because they knew Mother was a good cook and we lived on a farm. Most of them had been able at least once to fool us into believing he was our Rover.

Those hounds knew we always had fresh warm milk, and chickens if they got lucky and got into the hen house. There was no such thing as commercially prepared dog food in those days or if there was we sure couldn't afford to buy it, so all our Rovers ate table scraps.

You had to look Rover right in the eye to make sure you were feeding the right dog since they all looked alike and all would give you a sworn statement and swear they lived at our house so they could get farm-fresh meals.

Then I got married and my husband brought home a mongrel. He was mostly one of those flop-eared, sad-eyed basset hounds. Corkie was one of those dogs that could eat you out of house and home, go to three or four neighboring homes and do the same thing.

The trouble with Corkie was he was skinny. Worse than skinny—emaciated nearly. No matter how much he ate, he never gained weight. We got in trouble with some of those neighbors who were feeding him because he told the neighbors we never fed him. They would feel sorry for him, and he got another meal. I never figured out how he could hold so much food.

Then there was a dog we had for many years named Caesar. He came from a friend's litter of pups. I think we paid all of $5 for Caesar as a small pup when our youngest was a toddler. He could express himself very well. He would grow to become a huge black and white shaggy dog of dubious distinction but would have great vocal skills.

When Douglas got on his nerves as they were playing, or he became tired, the huge dog would lift his front paws onto our son's shoulders, put him on the ground and sit on Doug's legs with his feet up on Doug's shoulders. Looking him right in the eyes with a silly grin as he drooled over him, he told Doug to "leave me alone." There he would sit quite happily with his tongue lolling out one side of his mouth as he panted while our son screamed for us to get the dog off him. When we came running, Caesar would step off Doug's legs, and laughing merrily run away.

Caesar also loved watermelon. So did our youngest. I remember setting Douglas outside on the kitchen steps with a long slice of watermelon so he could spit the seeds out onto the ground.

When I went outside to check on him, there he sat eating from one end of the watermelon and Caesar eating contentedly on the other end. After that I always cut both of them a slice so they didn't have to share.

One day a neighbor's dogs came by and asked Caesar to follow him onto the nearby state park. Our property abutted the largest state park in Indiana and it would be our children's playground. Caesar went with the strays and when he found the superintendent's house at the park, he told the superintendent he was an orphan. The other two dogs were German shepherds and they would be penned in a cage until an owner came for them. But old Caesar had the run of the park since he was so tame and well behaved. They believed him and kept him and fed him from the barbeque pit for about a month until we found him. He had never eaten so well. He loved grilled hot dogs, never mind the relish or catsup, just give them to him straight and he was happy.

A friend told us where he was to be found and we went to pick him up. When we got there he told his new friends, "I have never seen them before in my life." His best pal, our youngest son, was hurt that he said that because it was a boldfaced lie. We loaded him in the back seat of the car. Caesar sat is the back seat crying and moaning, staring out the rear window back towards his new friends. I thought he was staring at his new friends, but it turned out he was probably staring at the barbeque pit. I was still not a very good cook and he remembered that fact very well.

Caesar looked a whole lot like a black bear and was nearly as large as one, so while he was on vacation at the state park he had quite an adventure. He hated thunderstorms and every window ledge on our house bore his nail prints gouged out in them where he had tried to get inside when it stormed.

Well, a big thunderstorm came one night while he was in the park and with nowhere to go he found a city dude's tent, went inside and made himself at home, sitting on this guy's chest. That city dude, who was spending his first night ever sleeping in a tent, woke up screaming, ran to the superintendent's office in his long underwear and said there was a bear in his tent and he wanted it shot. Of course, the superintendent didn't shoot Caesar, but he got inside for the night anyway. The dude said this was his first camping trip and I'm sure it probably would be his last as well.

But the best talking dogs we have ever had are the three we presently own. Two are beagle hounds and the third is a sheltie. Usually the sheltie, Jake, and the bowlegged beagle named Beau, pal around together. They ignore the other one, a red beagle named Goldie (go figure that one) who has golden eyes. But each of the beagles has a white tip on their tails.

I love to fish but being afraid of worms, I use bait called a "bee moth". It is a small white worm about an inch long, in fact about the length of the white tip of the dog's tails.

One day I called the dogs to come and eat supper. Beau sat down on her haunches,

Our dogs, Jake (the fuzzy one), Goldie (the fat one) and the pigeon toed Beau.

looked at me and I swear she was giggling. That is the only way I can explain her actions. She sat on her backside and using her front paws to slightly lift her back ones off the ground, she spun around on her fanny with her ears flying out from her body.

I asked her what was so funny and she told me she and Jake had been fishing. Now I doubted that very much but I asked her what they used as bait. Laughing wildly, she pointed to Goldie and said, "We used Goldie's tail."

She told me they caught a big catfish. "How did that happen?" I asked.

Beau explained that she and Jake had been playing on the dam of our pond when Goldie walked up and said she wanted to play too. We told her, "No, you can't. You have poop on your fur."

They then told her if she would go to the pond's overflow area and wash her fur they would play with her. She did, then like a dummy asked Beau and Jake how she could dry her fur. They told her to rub her backside on some green leaves nearby and she did.

About ten minutes later Goldie's belly started itching. It itched really badly. Those two mischievous dogs had talked her into rubbing her backside and underbelly on poison ivy leaves.

To make matters worse, after she continued to scratch and cry, they told her to put her hind end into the pond water and rub her belly in the muddy edge. This, they told her, would relieve the itching. She did as they advised and was getting really relaxed when, wham, bang, a big old catfish clamped down onto her tail thinking its white tip was a bee moth.

Well Jake and Beau each got hold of an ear and dragged Goldie from the mouth of that big catfish leaving it flopping on the dam, they said.

Poor Goldie, seeing how they were laughing at her, started to cry. I really felt sorry for her.

I then told the other two dogs that if they had a big fish lying out there on the dam to bring it in and I would cook it for their supper.

Beau and Jake took off, running madly toward the pond, then came back a few minutes later with that old hang-dog look on their faces, looking very embarrassed. They did not have that catfish.

They said, "It got away." I knew then they were lying hound dogs.

These instances I recall are the very reason I have determined you can't believe a word a dog says. I just don't understand how they can tell lies like this.

When I related this story to my sons, Lonnie reminded me about his fish story and how I didn't believe he caught a five pound bass when it swallowed a two pound bass. "And you expect me to believe this?" he queried.

Those Awful Ragweeds

As I was growing up in a small town in the middle of Southern Indiana I can remember my mother, and later my husband's grandmother, going out into the fields every spring with a bucket on their arm and a sharp knife in their hand.

As they took their walk through the fields they were gathering wild greens which they would cook for that evening's supper. These greens had colorful names such as lamb's tongue, white top, creeses (watercress), mustard, wild lettuce, sour dock, wild carrots, etc.

If you got a good mixture of the greens and cooked them all together until they were tender, then drained them they were ready for the skillet. Mother would fry up a small platter of home-cured bacon so she could have plenty of meat drippings for her greens. She would crumble the cooked bacon into small pieces, add the wilted greens and add salt and pepper.

Once on the plate you were encouraged to add a few drops of vinegar to enhance their flavor. I'm not sure how the vinegar worked but it did so I still use it on my greens.

As a kid I did not like green stuff. I was like most of the kids I knew. Green food was pretty gross, as the kids of today would say. I didn't like lettuce or cabbage no matter how you fixed the stuff.

I would be grown and married for many years before I became addicted to the green vegetables from our gardens. I say from our garden because if we have fresh greens on our table they will have come from our garden, not out in the wilds of the fields. There is a good reason for that.

When I got married I could not cook. Other than knowing how to bake cornbread, I could not fix a single dish. I could not make coffee. In fact I gave away three nice, very expensive Wearever aluminum coffeemakers before I determined it was not the pot but me. So for many years we used instant coffee. Folgers and Nescafe couldn't go wrong.

My husband's grandmother lived next door to us and for the first year or so she would bring down just enough food in a dish for him, never enough for the both of us. I guess she figured that if I wanted to eat I would learn to cook. That used to make me so mad, but the sorry excuse worked. I finally learned how to cook after many years of trial and error.

Today I am considered a pretty good cook.

But now, back to the ragweed story.

We had been married about three years and had two small sons. I was staying at home for a few months between jobs after the second son was born.

Being an eager young housewife wanting to please my husband, one day I decided to go into the field in front of our rental home while the babies took their naps and pick him some wild greens for supper.

Since I didn't know the names of any of the young shoots which were growing up in the field I determined to pick only one kind so I could be safe.

There were a lot of clumps about three or four inches tall. In fact, they were all over the field. Thinking to myself that here was a bounty, I decided to pick only those. They were very young and tender so I filled my grocery bag with the things.

I went back to the house and between taking care of the babies and cooking supper I cleaned those greens. I cleaned and cleaned and cleaned. Finally I decided I had enough to make a mess and put them on to cook. I threw the discarded pieces onto a compost heap outside.

Well, let me tell you, those greens sure didn't smell like any I had ever smelled cooking before. The longer they cooked the worse they smelled and the brighter green they became. By the time my husband came home from work the house reeked. That is the only way to describe the odor. A skunk running through the house wouldn't have left a worse odor.

"What are we having for supper tonight?" my husband warily asked me. He always seemed to look inside the cook pots or the oven to assess what I had fixed before he would actually consume anything I fixed.

So proud of myself I could nearly have burst, I told him about picking those greens and how young and tender they were.

He asked to see my discards. When he saw them he became hysterical with laughter. "Do you realize you have cooked all ragweeds," he asked?

Well, no, I did not know that fact. If they were young and green they should have been edible is the way I viewed things. I threw them out in disgust but I was determined to fix him a mess of greens.

The next week I went into that same field but I avoided all the ragweeds that had, by that time grown a lot taller. I picked only one kind again.

I took them into the house, cleaned and cooked them and they smelled really nice. When my husband came in that night he was sure I had done a good job finally. They smelled and looked just like what his Grandma used to fix he said. Bless my soul, I think he was actually bragging on me.

He placed a big helping of those greens on his plate, put a few drops of vinegar on them, wrapped a big wad around his fork and placed the savory bite into his mouth. I sat there expectantly, anticipating his big smile when he tasted the greens.

Instead of a smile, he immediately got a very strange look on his face, covered his mouth with his hands and ran outdoors to spit the greens out. That time I had cooked all sour dock and he informed me it was like eating a green persimmon. If you have never bitten into a green persimmon you are missing a treat. Let me get you one.

Since then when we want greens I go to his garden, or send him there, where they are planted in rows so I know what I am harvesting and get only those greens.

I have since learned a very good way to prepare greens. I carefully wash and remove the center rib from each leaf as I am washing it. When I get a big pot full I add about a quart and a half of water that when boiling will wilt the greens down nicely. After they have wilted all the way down as far as they will go, I sprinkle a heaping teaspoon of baking soda over them and immediately start stirring them around in the pot. If you take your eyes away from them for even a minute they will overflow the pot.

Let them cook about one minute after you add the soda then remove from the stove, pour the whole thing in the sink and run a lot of cold water over them, removing all the green foam. Keep doing this until the water runs clear.

While you are rinsing them, have a smaller pot on the stove to which you have added maybe a half-cup of olive oil; half of a medium coarsely chopped onion and salt to taste. When the onions are nearly opaque add about a ½ teaspoon of minced garlic (I use dried garlic and it works fine). Cook about 1 minute more then add the greens. Let them cook until they are completely tender, about 20 minutes.

This same recipe can be used on about all kinds of greens. If I run out of my own home grown greens, I buy a one pound package of frozen spinach at the grocery and prepare them in this manner. If I need more moisture while the frozen ones defrost, I add about 1/3 cup of white wine.

The first time I cooked them like this my husband came in and said, "Whew, what's that smell. It smells awful." I agree it does smell awful. After he tasted them his tune changed though to, "How can something that smells that awful taste so good?"

You might want to try this recipe also.

One other green I have fixed for my husband for which he thought I was trying to poison him the first time I served it is fried polk or "poke." We always pronounced it poke.

Harvest only the leaves and the upper parts of the stalk when the polk plant is very young. Wash carefully under running water and chop coarsely. Add about a 1/3-cup of cornmeal and salt and pepper to taste. Mix well and place in a well-oiled medium hot skillet and fry until fairly crisp, turning often to keep them from burning.

This is a surprisingly good spring taste treat. It is one we brought to Indiana from Kentucky. Most people in Indiana like to use only the leaves and boil it until it is done, seasoning with salt and pepper to taste and adding some meat drippings to the water. I am OK with fixing it this way, but I prefer it fried.

The polk root, berries and the larger stalks are said to be poison, but the tender young shoots and leaves have never hurt us. Until you become accustomed to eating it each year, you should eat only small amounts until your body acclimates itself to the new food.

My husband now accepts eating fried poke as a rite of spring in our house. The same greens chopped and bagged can be frozen in your freezer and used year round with good results.

One other ritual of spring is making the family a pot of hot sassafras tea. The Kentucky old timers said it was a good purge for ridding one's body of all the toxins of winter.

They would go into the woods or along a fence row and dig up the root of small sassafras. The root should be washed thoroughly. Trim the bark from the root and with a sharp knife draw downward against the root, cutting small chunks of the root to be used for tea.

It doesn't take many three-inch pieces of this pungent root to make about a gallon of tea. Place the cut pieces in a gallon pot of water. Bring to a near boil, but do not let it boil. Heat just to boiling but do not let it boil, turn the heat down to a simmer, keeping a lid on the pot. Steep slowly for about a half-hour. Serve hot, plain or with cream and sugar.

Today some restaurants serve this tea iced, but I have never liked it like that. If you let it boil instead of steep, it will get very bitter and ruin the flavor.

During the Depression years, the harvesting, bunching and selling of small "hands" of sassafras roots to peddlers and other buyers of roots, kept many families from starving to death. The income derived from this practice was, for many, their only income.

Mickey is leaning on a tree stump looking out over the water as he snared suckers.

Suckers and Mushrooms

Spring is a wonderful time of year. New leaves are crisp and shiny, poison ivy is not quite a hindrance yet, mushrooms are growing and suckers are running.

What is a mushroom and what is a sucker that runs one might ask. Most people know what a mushroom is, especially the morels. It grows along the forest floor under certain kinds of trees and is considered a real delicacy by many. I'll explain about suckers that run and swim a little later on in the story.

You have to find morel mushrooms fast because they are only around about three weeks or so in the spring, then the frost line moves north a little more each day and so do the mushrooms. Enjoy them while you can is the country motto.

Beginning about the second or third week in April until about the second week in May the woods are open territory to one and all as cars are parked alongside the roadways and people wander into the woods to hunt the elusive sponge.

There are two or three kinds of morels. There are the gray or black as some call them, the big yellows and the false morels. Both the grays and yellows are good to eat but some say not to eat the false morels. I have eaten them with no damage to my system but if you are unsure, do not eat one.

The grays are generally pretty small and arrive earlier than their cousins, the yellows, are not over three inches or so in height and very hard to find. The big yellows are much larger and a little easier to find if you first acclimate your eyes to what you are looking for. Finding the first one may take you a while, but after that it becomes somewhat easier.

What is wonderful about mushrooms is sometimes they grow in pretty dense patches and you can pick a bunch without a lot of effort. I have only been lucky like that one time and it was a real thrill. Usually though they will be scattered over hillsides near and far and only under certain kinds of trees. Since I don't know but about two kinds of trees I cannot tell you which trees they grow best under. My husband swears by rotten elm trees. He looks under ash, elm, sycamore and poplar. You sometimes have to walk for miles up one hill and down another to find enough for a mess.

But to hear some of the more blatant, I won't call them liars, tale tellers tell about finding mushrooms in patches you might want to doubt their veracity. Sometimes they just tell you that to get you into the woods for a walk and to exercise yourself.

If a mushroom hunter shows you a grocery bag of the delicious fungi and then tells you WHERE he found them you KNOW he is lying. No one tells you where his favorite patch of woods is found. He will swear he found every one of those things under one tree in so-and-so's woods. You go there and look. You won't find one, not even the remaining white stems will be apparent, I guarantee that, but it will probably mean a long walk for you to find that certain tree. But, if you want mushrooms badly enough, you will be more than eager to make that long trek to where you were told you would find them. I can just see the tale teller sitting back laughing because you believed him.

Mickey after a successful mushroom hunt

I remember one time a co-worker of mine asked my husband and me to take her and her husband and father-in-law mushroom hunting. She would provide us a well-filled picnic basket and iced tea to enjoy when we returned to our car, she said. That sounded pretty fine and since my husband loved to walk and hunt mushrooms he agreed.

The day he took us started out very nice. My friend Trish removed her sweatshirt and tied the thing around her waist not long into the trek. The longer we walked the hotter it got that day and it became very, very humid. We walked about three hours and were absolutely drenched with sweat when we finally saw the light at the end of the tunnel. Our vehicle was in sight and so was that iced tea. Our throats were parched.

We rushed to the car, unloaded the picnic supplies and Trish poured each of us a big glass of iced tea. I took a drink, spat it out and started chasing her screaming, "I am going to kill you, you little witch."

As she ran for her very life she finally got me to tell her what was wrong. She had made iced tea with cinnamon flavored tea bags. Now normally that might not have been too bad but I absolutely hate flavored teas of any kind and I was so thirsty I could have died. I don't think I ever forgave her for that.

But we found a lot of mushrooms that day. I came home and sliced them lengthwise and ran them under cold running water then placed the halves in salt water to soak the bugs and leaf mold out of them.

After rinsing the salt water off the next day, I rolled them in flour, salt and pepper and sautéed them in a hot skillet of butter until they were crisp.

So I guess the trip was all right. But I don't think we ever took her mushroom hunting again.

The summer before our son Doug started college he experimented with preserving morels for later use. Several weeks after he left I found one lying on the range hood in the kitchen, dried to a crisp. Curious, I placed it in water and in minutes it sprang back to life. From then on I dehydrated any excess morels that the guys found and brought home. They are delicious.

To dehydrate a morel you do not want to soak them first in salt water; that will ruin them and they will turn black as coal.

Slice the morels in two lengthwise and hold under gently running water to remove any woods debris or spiders. Let them dry normally for an hour or so then arrange them in a dehydrator tray. My dehydrator has six big trays so I can do a lot at one time. Set the thermostat at 145 degrees and leave it running for about an hour or two. Once dried they can be placed in a plastic bag and put in the freezer or into a cloth bag and hung in a closet.

To rehydrate them, place as many as you want into a pan of warm, not hot water. Leave them for five minutes or so and change the water again. Let them stand in warm water until completely rehydrated then prepare as usual. Their texture and taste will be the same as fresh picked.

At the start of this story I mentioned suckers. And for those of you who haven't a clue what a sucker is I will explain.

A sucker is a fresh water fish akin to the carp family. It is usually either a "redhorse" or a "blackhorse" or white sucker. The red and white sucker has large scales like the carp, but the black one has small scales and is better to eat. All have many bones you must score with a knife. Scoring means cutting through to the skin on the meaty side every 1/8-inch or so to disable the bones and make the fish fit to eat. My husband and his family loved the things, but I have never liked fish. I guess I was afraid of swallowing a bone and having it lodge in my throat.

They swim up small shallow running creeks to spawn about the same time as the mushrooms are being found and make a good side dish to eat with the mushrooms. With another side of cooked greens and a pan of cornbread you can have a nice meal.

People used to "gig" for suckers. They would carry a gunnysack attached to their belt or back somehow by a strap in which to place the fish. The hunters would go into the creeks at night with a powerful spotlight in one hand or attached to their head by a helmet harness and a gig in their other hand. A gig is a dangerous weapon. It has up to five very sharp barbed tines on the end that are about three inches long attached to a long pole.

When a sucker was spotted, the gig would be thrown and the prize impaled fish placed into the sack. The hunt would go on until the fisherman had all that he wanted or all that he could carry on his back.

Lonnie, his grandfather Don Ayers and his cousin, Penny, hold some of the fish that were caught by snaring.

The suckers weren't very valuable as food fish but they were fun to catch. But valuable or not, they became very important staples in the diet of poor families.

In later years, after the state declared the practice of gigging illegal, someone got the bright idea to put a copper noose on the end of a long cane pole and hook the fish when it swam through the noose. Copper was used because it was soft and could be seen easily under the water and could be guided by the fisherman. The noose would be weighted down with a very heavy metal washer or hollow stone so it could be maneuvered through the running water.

This kind of fishing was legal. I guess the state didn't realize just how accurate a noose could be. It had to be done in daylight and only in certain local creeks to be legal.

The person holding the snare would place the loop right in front of or behind the fish and then work it around the fish without touching the fish or letting it become aware of its probable fate. The minute the fish was within the noose the pole would be jerked upward and the sucker slung toward the creek bank or the gravel bar. Someone would remove the fish and put it on a stringer, open the snare again and the person working the pole went back to work.

I remember one year that the fishers in a local creek caught about 1,000 pounds of suckers. They filled a lot of freezers that year.

There was one older man who came to the creek every day. The guys would take turns snaring in the best spots while those above worked as spotters and alerted the fisherman when one was coming.

This one guy, who usually showed up about half snookered on beer, wanted to take his place one day and it was agreed he could. He was a regular with the crowd and had provided them with a lot of laughs at his expense over the years. Most of the time he provided us laughs with his driving. He drove in spurts. Going on a beer run, he would first push the accelerator, then back off, then push it again, and back off, doing this for the entire 30-mile round trip.

Our son, Lonnie, swears he saw Doyle doing 70 miles per hour one time and not moving forward an inch. I don't doubt his word one bit. The guys had been cutting wood and Doyle had gotten his car stuck because he said it was "whipsawing" on him as he tried to drive forward. Doyle repeated himself over and over as he spoke so this came out as "whipsawing, yup, whipsawing," etc. He kept spinning his tires uselessly until the guys finally felt sorry for him and gave him a boost.

On this day at the creek bank Doyle was standing on a fallen log and we tried to get him wet. One of the bystanders would say, "Come on, Doyle, there's one headed your way." He would lean out from that log as far as he could and reach out still further with his pole.

He couldn't even see the fish but the one directing would tell him how to move his noose. "Just a little farther," they would say. Doyle finally caught on to what was about to happen and slung the pole down and came ashore. "I know what you guys are trying to do. You want to see me get wet, yup, you guys want to get me wet." Sometimes he got wet but most of the time he would sober up enough to realize what they were doing.

Everyone would have a good laugh, even Doyle, and someone else would take his place on the fallen log or on a nearby gravel bar.

We had a lot of fun over the years snaring those fish out of the creek. You could see cars lined up along the creek for several evenings with men staring into the water until someone spotted the suckers "running" or swimming upstream to spawn. Then the call would go out. The next day would see the creek bank lined with spotters and fishermen.

Nowadays it doesn't seem like people do these kinds of things very much. I guess the ones who did it are now mostly dead and gone. When you want to eat fish it is easier to go to a fish house and order them already fixed for the table.

But that takes all the fun out of it.

Cooking Like a Kentuckian

In writing this book I have given you many recipes for fixing foods for your families that are exactly the way the Kentuckians and the hillbillies living in Southern Indiana prepared them. You now know how to catch and fry fish; hunt, preserve and cook mushrooms; grow or pick from the wild several kinds of greens. You know how to make your own hominy, how to cure and cook several kinds of meats; how to render lard and make cornbread.

With the following recipe for making your own butter to spread on that cornbread you will know as much about mountain cooking as I know.

To make butter you should own a good milk cow or buy from a nearby farm, three or four gallons of fresh whole milk. Strain the milk through a paper-lined sieve to remove any impurities. Place the milk in large mouth gallon jars and set it in the refrigerator to cool. The cream will rise to the top of the milk in a couple of hours. Remove that cream with a large spoon and place the cream in a churn or jar. Leave the jar of cream on the kitchen countertop until soured, usually about three or four hours.

Once it is soured, start shaking, dashing or mixing the cream. I own a Daisy one gallon churn as well as a tall dasher type stone churn. The butter will quickly start appearing in the jar as yellow clots. Once you have a lot of these yellow clots, remove them with a slotted spoon and place them in a good-sized bowl. The remaining mixture is known as buttermilk and is a taste treat in itself and should be drunk when it is icy cold. Hold the bowl containing the yellow clots under running cold water as you work the clots around with the spoon, removing any milk residue, gathering the clots until they stay together in a clump.

Still stirring, salt the butter lightly if desired, or leave it unsalted. Place the cleaned butter in a bowl, cover and refrigerate until needed. If you are lucky enough to have a butter "mold" place your butter in that and when it is inverted out of the bowl onto a plate there will be a pretty design on the bottom of the butter.

I look back now at how jealous I was of my friends who did not live on a farm or have access to freshly churned butter. I was so envious. We had to eat that old cow butter. Theirs always came in nice rectangular sticks that were so neat, I thought. Nowadays that fresh butter sounds pretty good to me and I think how foolish I was to be envious of my friends who were probably, in their turn, envious of me for having what I had and took for granted.

You are now well prepared to fix some meals for your family that are fit for any king. Get into that kitchen and start rattling those pots and pans. Don't forget to invite me to sample your wares when you have them ready.

I'll bring along the dessert of freshly baked gingerbread men made from my own sorghum when I come to your house.

Grapevine Swings

A country kid can have fun with anything and along with having fun can actually earn a little bit of spending money.

We never had to "entertain" our kids as they were growing up. We never heard of setting up "play dates" with other children. We lived so far out in the country from any town they were best friends to each other and wherever one was you could be sure the other was there also. If they had not had each other, both of them would have been very lonely. If one couldn't think of something to do the other one did.

They loved the woods and streams of the Brown County State Park in Southern Indiana. We lived most of their growing up years on the south edge of it so the park was their playground. They could spend hours in those woods. They were impaired in adventure only by their imagination.

When they were pretty small yet I worked at the Atterbury Job Corps Center which was just getting a good start. This was another part of the president's war on poverty program. Every day more furniture was unpacked and placed into offices near me. I would bring home carloads of empty boxes for the boys to play with. I'll bet people wondered why I took so many of those boxes home with me. If they would fit into my car, they went home with me. Security even stopped me one night and searched my car. All they found were those empty boxes. I explained to the security personnel how my kids loved big boxes. From then on I could have taken any item I wanted to steal in if it had been placed in one of the big boxes. When security saw me coming, they would just wave me through with a smile. I guess they had children of their own and recognized my story as the truth.

Our two boys never needed or wanted expensive electronic toys to play with either. Had any been developed by the time they were of an age to play with them they might have wanted them, but they were just not available yet. They were satisfied with those boxes things came in. One would sit in the box and the other would drag him along the smoothly finished basement floor in a big circle. They would take turns doing this until the big box disintegrated. Then they grabbed another box and the fun started all over again.

Some of them would become playhouses, or clubhouses as they liked to call them, and would be placed either in a corner of the basement or out in the garage and that was their area in which to stay, visit, tell stories and make up mischief ideas. When they were in their house, we left them alone to play. They were safe and could improve upon their imagination and knowledge.

They loved to go for rides with us in our old Willys Jeep they had helped their dad restore. We would ride on the trails in the state park. Once when we were quite a ways into the woods our youngest said, "Mick (the boys always called their dad by his first name), we have to turn left here."

"How do you know that," he asked our six-year-old son.

"We play back here all the time," he responded.

After hearing that comment and realizing just how far from home they were I became worried. After all they were only maybe six and eight years old at the time. So I found a set of walkie-talkies for $15 at the local drugstore and bought them. They guaranteed a range of ¼ mile but we could hear coon hunters on them as far away as Georgia and hear air traffic controllers talking to airliners.

Each time they wanted to go into the woods to play they were required to take one of the instruments with them on their belt. I kept the other. They were never to separate in the woods. When I wanted them to come home I would talk into my instrument. If they were too far away to hear my voice, they could hear the static when the microphone was activated and would know that I wanted them home. Soon they would come running off the hillside into home.

One of their favorite things to do while playing in the woods was to swing from grapevines.

They would find one attached firmly to a large tree next to a ravine. Pulling one end loose from the tree they then had a swing. The would grab their end, run backwards a few steps and then rush forward, finally lifting off and over the ravine with their feet drawn up below them, giving their full throated Tarzan yells as they had seen him do on television movies, landing safely on the other side.

I learned somewhat later in life that they and some neighborhood children liked to double up on the swings. One would swing out over the ravine and one would grab hold of a tree limb on the opposite side staying there. The other would return the swing back to the waiting children for the next one to grab. That one would swing out, and the one holding onto the limb would grab onto the others' body and be "rescued."

This had gone on many times when one day the neighbor boy took a swing over the ravine and suddenly lost his grip about half way across. He fell for a good long way, screaming all the way down. Several of the children ran home and told their brothers and sisters of the injured boy. His parents and older siblings went in search of the injured Tarzan. He had a broken leg but other than that he was OK.

A few weeks in a cast and he was as good as new. My kids returned home and I never heard them even mention this other kid.

Sometimes I'm glad my kids didn't tell me everything they got up to in those woods.

With the energy of only the young they would run down their side of the ravine or find another vine, run up the other side and do it all over again. Hours could be spent playing Tarzan of the Jungle.

Sometimes, too, they would find a fairly tall, springy sapling, climb to its top and ride it to the ground then dismount letting the tree revert to its erect status. They thought it was great fun for a large kid and a small kid to ride the tree down at the same time. When it reached the bottom, the larger kid would let go, forcing the other kid to either hang on and ride it back up, or let loose and fall to the ground.

Other times they would practice swinging down from the tops of tall trees like Tarzan did, swinging from limb to limb. If I went outside to look for them, I generally had to look into the tree canopy and see which tree was swaying the most. That's where they would be.

In those days they were as lithe and sleek as a white-tailed deer. There wasn't an ounce of fat on their bodies; their stomach muscles looked like a washboard they were so tightly muscled.

While in the woods they would keep their eyes open for moneymaking opportunities also. At a very early age they learned to look into the tops of the trees for bittersweet. This was a small vine which had pea-sized orange balls on it in the fall. When ripe, the balls would open into a small flower, exposing a deep orange berry inside. Bunches of this vine could be sold in their roadside stand and accounted for quite a lot of their money. It was used as home décor and was a valuable commodity for the boys.

They also looked around ponds in the park and nearby ponds for cattail weeds. Those could be cut when brown and ripe, sprayed with hairspray or spray enamel and sold when dried for a nickel each in their roadside stand.

They looked closely for ginseng too. This very expensive root was the source of a lot of their funds. The roots were dug, cleaned, dried and sold to ginseng dealers. They once found a root that had a large piece in the center and two prongs on either end of it that weighed almost a full pound. My husband who had been with them that particular day overlooked the plant, thinking it was a small tree sapling. Lonnie, our oldest boy, recognized it for what it was and dug the root.

The ginseng buyer was very impressed with the size and notified Lonnie he was going to dry it a little further and would send him a nice check soon. He did. I think Lonnie got about $60 for that one root. Today it would probably be worth $300-$400.

Mickey says he was taught by his elderly cousin Gentry Robertson how to recognize ginseng. Another older friend, Ansel Hillenburg, taught him that ginseng could be found more often on north and east facing hillsides since they were a shade loving plant, but the largest root Mickey ever saw was actually found on a south facing slope. This was the one Lonnie recognized. Mickey had thought it was a hickory tree root.

To aid the boys in their moneymaking schemes my husband built them a small rickety shelter alongside the state road near our house. There was a pull over there where cars could stop safely. It was there that the boys made a killing selling extra produce from our garden and the treasures found in their beloved woods to the tourists.

I had to scour every pond for miles around cutting cattails. The pond owners were delighted with my efforts at clearing their ponds of these weeds. The boys climbed trees and pulled the bittersweet down and bunched it for sale. They also sold all our excess vegetables from the garden. They knew where every hickory and walnut tree grew in the area. They would pick up the nuts, brown bag them and sell those to the tourists.

I remember one year we bought a 25-cent package of gourd seed. We planted those seeds and installed a small fence on which the vines could twine. We picked 11 bushes of various sized and colored gourds from that 25 cents worth of seed. The boys sold the gourds as fall table decorations for five cents each or six for a quarter. Most people bought at least a quarter's worth.

One day they came running to the house to tell us of an experience they had had down at their stand. An older couple had stopped by their stand to see what they had to sell. There stood the boys, about 6 and 8 at that time in their un-hemmed cut off jean shorts with raveled strings hanging down their very dirty brown legs, with their bare feet and sweaty faces. And knowing these two boys as I did, I can imagine them talking the legs off everyone who stopped to chat and buy from them. Lonnie was always a talker and could have sold ice cream to Eskimos.

The elderly lady said to her husband, "Oh, Henry, aren't they cute. Let's buy something." And buy they did. About $5 worth. That was a fortune to those kids.

Both those country "boys" are now grown men. They travel the world consulting with global sized companies who pay dearly for their expertise. They are still very much down to earth and earn far more than they could have made in their little roadside stand. I sometimes wonder what their sophisticated customers would think if the boys suddenly started telling them about bittersweet wreaths and grapevine swings.

No matter how much the boys earned at their roadside stand it would not have been enough to pay for all the hospital visits to get stitches, casts, e-rays and other such things. They were always getting hurt, not because they were careless necessarily but because they were always in the thick of anything that went on.

Doug's head got mellowed at an early age when he fell from the moving pickup truck and struck the roadway. The door to the old truck had come open as Mickey drove up a steep curving bank near our house and Doug fell out onto the highway. That would be the first of six brain concussions he would receive and Lonnie got one the first day of his sixth grade year. He earned his badge and stitches when a classmate let a baseball bat slip out of his hands while batting at a ball and the flying bat struck Lonnie across the top of his head.

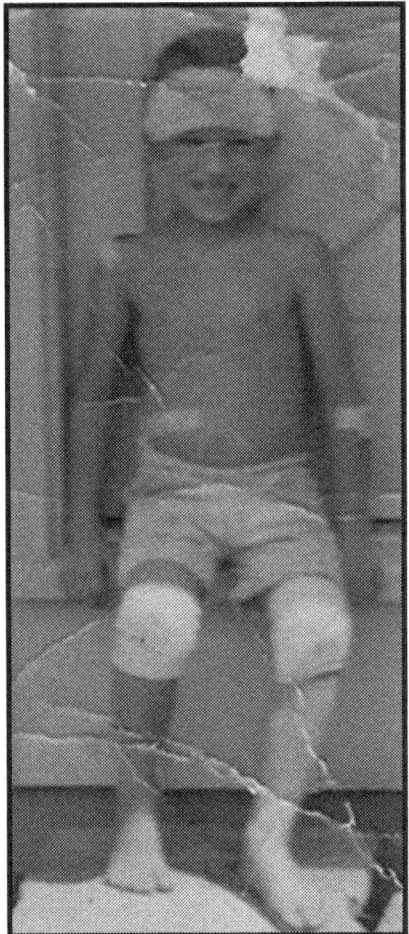

Doug in bandages after falling from the pickup truck.

Lonnie would have several broken bones or dislocated joints over the years and Doug was forever getting his head injuries, which always required an overnight stay at the local hospital. It seemed to me that they were always getting hurt somehow or another.

One time on the way home from the baby-sitter's house, Doug had gotten carsick and puked inside my car. As soon as

I got home I put him to bed and took a bucket of soapy water to the car to clean it. Before I crossed the road to the car, I re-started the wringer washer machine so it could be running while I worked. I had no more gotten to the other side of the road to the car when I heard Lonnie screaming. He had tried to "help" me with the laundry and the wringer grabbed his right arm. By the time I got back to where he was his arm was in that wringer clear to the shoulder.

This is about the way things went at our house in the course of a day. If you have ever had children of your own I'm sure you recognize yourself in these stories.

I was never as blasé about it as Mother had been with us. I could not always fix things with a clean sheet and a pan of warm, soapy Lysol water. The injuries the boys got were very serious. I finally became an emergency medical technician (EMT) just so I would be able to see them injured without panicking.

Did it keep me from panicking? No. But at least I got to where I could recognize serious blood from not so serious blood.

Mick and TNT

It seems there was always a guy in every neighborhood that was familiar with the use of dynamite. In our neighborhood, it was my husband, Mickey. He thoroughly enjoyed handling the stuff.

Anytime someone needed something blasted; they came to him for assistance. Maybe they wanted a dry well blasted, or a stump removed, etc. He was their man.

It started I believe in his young days when he was working for his brother-in-law as a water well driller way back in the early 1950's. His brother-in-law was a real chicken about stuff like dynamite and many other things as well. Whenever a well driller drilled a dry well, the old-time well diggers would tie a stick or two of dynamite on a fuse and string, lower it down in the well, get behind a tree and set it off.

It was believed that if you disturbed the rock layers enough, water would come in through the cracks you made. I don't know if this helped, but Mickey had a good time trying. He has always loved to blast things. It was always his heartfelt belief that if a little dynamite did good, a whole lot did better.

He had a job working on the county roads and bridges in the mid 1960's when the federal government was building the Monroe Reservoir to serve as a water source for the city of Bloomington.

After the homes and farms that would later be affected by the rising water levels had been purchased and torn down, the federal government got a really bright idea. They would spend several million dollars to construct bridges over several creeks to build a road that went nowhere and ended in the middle of a creek. No bridge would be built there, but several would be built along the way before the road ended in the creek. Now had this road served any real purpose I would have been all for it, but it didn't.

That was fine. Boy, we could just speed along that road for several miles, then whoops, apply the brakes boys, the road ends right here.

But Mickey had a good job working on the road and we really needed the money at the time. Although his job title was laborer, once his bosses knew he liked to set off dynamite, one of his duties was to blast tree stumps and rocks out of the way of the rest of the equipment.

Once he kept planting a little bit of the big booming stuff, using only a few sticks of dynamite, under a particularly big stump. The dynamite would go boom, jar the stump a bit, and then the stump would settle right back where it had grown.

This went on for several tries on his part until he got the bright idea to put a whole case of dynamite under this stump. He had the guy on the excavator dig a bigger hole under the tree roots, pushed that big bunch of sticks under the stump and told everyone to take cover. I don't image he had to tell his co-workers twice. They were beginning to know him pretty well by this time.

When the dynamite exploded that time it threw house-size boulders high into the air. To save his own life, he crawled under a large piece of earth moving machinery as a huge rock came down to earth right where he had been standing, but the stump was removed.

Another man had hidden inside a big heavy wooden crate the dynamite had arrived in. He stayed inside the crate so long they thought he had been killed. It turned out he was afraid to come out with my husband with his hands full of dynamite still on the scene.

Work continued until that little project was done.

He also worked for a bridge crew. It wasn't his job specifically to handle the dynamite, but it seemed he was the one always doing the blasting. On one bridge he blew a big stump out and along with a few rocks, it came right down into the windshield of our only old car. We really needed that car at the time but with a front seat filled with dirt, mud, broken glass and a tree stump, it was kind of crowded in there.

Now our family, another brother-in-law, aunt and uncle, and a cousin's husband worked together for several months to build each of us a new house. We each bought our own materials and the others got together and helped build the houses.

The cousin's house needed a well. They had a big diameter well that had been dug by a backhoe but it would go dry in the summer so they decided to dig it deeper. The only problem was the backhoe could not help them; it couldn't get through the rocks. So, you guessed it, they asked my husband to blast the rocks.

This time he was prepared, he thought. The cousin's husband rented a jackhammer and drilled some holes deep into the rock at the bottom of the well. My husband planted the dynamite, a lot of dynamite, in those holes.

To keep down the debris, they got another brilliant idea and dumped old tires into the hole prior to the blast to hold the broken rocks down.

Everyone took cover and Mickey set off the dynamite. Those tires looked like tiny donuts or lifesavers flying high into the air. I don't believe they ever found any of them.

Later that day the cousin went back to her mobile home parked nearby where they had been living while they built their new house. When she entered her home there was a big hole through the roof, ceiling, kitchen table and partially through the floor under the table. Embedded in the floor was this huge stone, blown from their well. It had missed a coffee cup full of cold brew on its way down through the house.

In later years the federal government placed so many restrictions on who could and could not get access to dynamite (a smart move on their part I think) that my husband finally gave up his fun side-line occupation. It has been several years now since he got to play with dynamite. I sometimes think he misses the fun. He still loves to tell the grandkids about his adventures.

My Dad had had very similar experiences with dynamite. He worked for many years as a blaster in the coalmines; setting sticks to blast the coal from the veins after which it would be shoveled into coal cars then taken to the tipples. He loved to holler, "Fire in the Hole." That was the term used by miners to let the other workers know dynamiting was eminent and they should take cover. So Mickey and Dad had quite a lot in common.

Final Goodbyes

Final goodbyes can be very emotional and difficult to get through. I know. I have been through several myself and even though I know the loved one is now in a better place, it was nearly impossible to let them go. It takes time to get to the healing stage and realize that yes, they are indeed in a better place.

But go they must and so will we when our time comes. I have been very close to death twice in the past few years, but survived to tell the tale. It had been so difficult when our mother and dad each died that when the doctors told my husband to notify our sons that I might be nearing death I asked him not to do that.

I would have loved seeing them one last time but I also wanted them to remember me as they had last seen me, happy and healthy. Usually I am very upbeat, ditzy and caring about their welfare. I did not want them to be there if I really had to pay my tab and check out of this world. I can't remember if I ever told them just how sick I had been after I had gotten better. But I probably did because often when we close a conversation we tell each other 'I love you."

I only know that the first time I thought I would die I knew in my heart I had something I had to take care of first. I had come awake that morning, three days after surgery, to find there was a little man with big ears, about a foot and a half tall, clothed in a white dress with his feet stuck behind him, tooting music on some kind of horn.

I kept telling my nurses the "Spirit Collector" was bobbing around on the ceiling in the corner of the room behind my bed.

I didn't know then and I still don't know why I always referred to him as "the Spirit Collector", but I knew that is who he was, that was his name, and that is what he did. He collected spirits.

He stayed with me for about a day and a half. The nurses became alarmed when I described what I was seeing. They did not doubt I really was seeing something they said, but told me they could not see him themselves.

"When I woke up I realized I was down in that flute of a thing," I told them. "There was a bunch of people's heads going further and further back into the corner, all telling me to "Go back, Go back. If he puts his thumb over that and you're in there, you will be dead." I didn't want that to happen so I got back into my bed and nurses ran in and took my temperature. It was just under 106 degrees. An ice bath was forthcoming, but it didn't do a thing to remove the little man playing his music. He continued to play that horn. It drove me crazy. He kept playing the same song over and over but I never knew what song he was playing. What I at first thought of as a flute was a misconception because a flute is played by holding the flute to one side. He blew straight into this thing. And his big ears I later realized were not his ears at all but the top fold of his white wings.

That night was Christmas Eve. I knew in my mind there was an unfinished project on my mind. The only phone number I could remember kept going around and around inside my head. I was too sick to look up anyone's number and at that point probably would not have known how to even find the telephone book. I just grabbed the phone and dialed that repeating number.

A man answered and I asked him who he was. He told me his name and then it all came back to me what I had yet to do before I died.

"Michael, I am in the hospital and may die. The veteran's memorial we have been working on needs the names updated. Will you finish that for me if I die?" I asked him. We had worked together for about two years completing a monument to our county's veterans. Just before I had become sick I had written an article in the local newspaper asking for other names to add to the memorial. That story had come out the day I was admitted to the hospital and the letters were mounting up.

Michael had not known until then that I was even sick. He told me I was very lucky I reached him. He had been ready to walk out the door to attend Christmas Eve church services, he told me.

"Helen," he said, "You are going to be all right. I am on my way to church right now and I am going to turn this over to a higher power." He did. The next morning, for the first time in 17 days, my temperature was less than 105 degrees. My doctor told me that if it went below 102 for two days I could go home. A few days later it dropped to 101 and I returned home to recuperate for eight more years.

It took me a long, long time to get back my health; in all, over eight years. I remained on high-powered antibiotics for five years after returning home after having 196 transfusions of liquid antibiotics at the hospital.

During the time I was at home recuperating I had two more experiences where guardian angels came to me. I rose from my bed, I thought, one morning and walked into my living room. There on the couch sat my mother and dad, and mother's brother Henry and his wife, Bertha. "What are all you guys doing in my living room?" I asked. "You are all dead and I just about was myself," I told them.

Mother replied, "Yes, Helen, we know that but we have been back here looking after you quite a bit lately."

Then the four of them disappeared, never to be seen again, but I know I have four guardian angels somewhere out there. I woke, realizing I had been dreaming again. Or had I?

Another time I awoke from a dream (I thought) to find someone was holding me by the back of my neck and we were flying through the air at a tremendous speed. In fact, the speed was so fast it was very noisy. I realized it was the end of time and yelled for them to pick up my husband. "Don't worry," they replied. "Someone else has already picked him up." "But what about those kids down there, aren't you going to get them?" "No," they told me sadly, "the kids of today are so mean that very few of them will get into heaven." Then I woke up for real.

Almost five years ago I nearly died again but survived total kidney and respiratory failure. My oxygen level was only 57% when I was admitted to the hospital, which was nearly unheard of. The doctors again did not think I would live or that I would not have major brain damage if I did live. But I know in my heart my four guardian angels pulled me through again. I really do keep them busy I guess.

Shortly after I became ill the first time I ordered some new clothing for myself because I was too ill to shop in stores. When I opened the packages there was an angel pin included in the order. I pinned it to the lapel of one of my new jackets and thought no more about it. The next three times I ordered items by mail there was another different angel pin enclosed at no charge to me. I now have one to wear on each of my jackets and I keep those little guys busy.

Recently my husband and I were traveling about 20 miles from home when we met a semi loaded down with frozen crossties. Each crosstie weighed an average of 250 pounds. Within three to five seconds after we met the truck, it accidentally lost its load in front of us. They were pouring from the bed of his truck toward us in unbelievable numbers and very fast. Within seconds it was over. All but three or four of those ties falling onto the roadway either fell flat, slid off the road or otherwise missed our windshield and our heads. The last few that fell were falling into those already crowded on the roadway so they bounced and flew end over end over our car. The very last one fell straight down through the passenger side front fender and bumper then fell flat to the side of the road. That bumper damage was the only damage to our vehicle. Had even one of the approximately 120 crossties come through our windshield we could and probably would have been decapitated.

After we left our vehicle I became chilled, I suppose from the shock of realizing we could very easily have been killed. My knees started shaking and I sat back down in the seat, reached into the back seat for my jacket, and sure enough there was an angel pin on its lapel. I told my husband about the angel pins showing up in my packages. "Do you always wear one?" he asked me. I assured him I always wore one on each of my jackets. "Well, keep it there," he replied.

I do not know who sent me the pins. They just began showing up, right when I needed them!

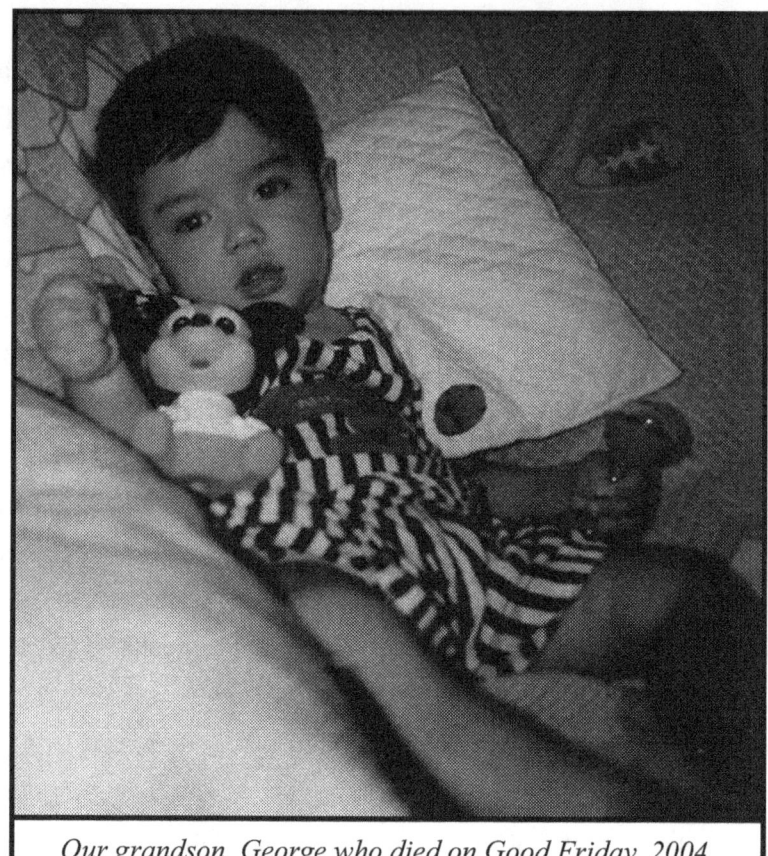

Our grandson, George who died on Good Friday, 2004.

The death of our mother and dad and my best friend were the first deaths of those close to me. Mother died in 1982, my friend in 1984 and Dad in 1986. We have also lost sisters-in-law Barbara, Dorothy and Clara and a brother-in-law, David; our grandson, George; a niece, Misty; and Sylvia lost a baby at birth she named Greg.

Our niece Misty died after she had been bitten by a brown recluse spider. Even though she was a severely handicapped Down's Syndrome child, she added a dimension to all our lives we would not have believed possible. Her death required me to write a poem and read it at her funeral. I say, "required" because I truly believe if I had not written it and gotten those words down on paper I would never have slept again. I tried to deny writing it the first day it popped into my head and didn't sleep a wink that night until after 3 a.m. Usually I am asleep by 9 p.m. at the latest. So after her wake I sat at my computer and five minutes later it was finished.

That night I got to sleep without any problems. I read the poem the next day during her funeral surprising not only the other family members but also myself. I sang the last two lines, which are included in the song "May the Good Lord Bless and Keep You 'Til We Meet Again."

My sister Sylvia said, "I didn't know you were going to sing that." "I didn't know it either," I replied, but something compelled me to do that. My performance and the words of the poem brought acclaim from my husband who usually is not appreciative of poetry. "That was really nice," he told me.

I will include that poem at the end of this story.

When mother entered the hospital for a simple gallbladder surgery, she never returned. She had been in terrible pain and even though the doctors had told her several years prior to that that she had terminal cirrhosis of the liver we never expected the gallbladder surgery to kill her.

Actually, she came through the surgery fine. She was just in a terrible lot of pain, so the doctors ordered a pain killing shot for her. I do not know what kind they gave her but it threw her into a coma because her liver was almost totally non-functional because of her disease. She had always been so embarrassed to tell anyone she had cirrhosis. She had always associated that disease with a person being an alcoholic and she never drank. In actuality, cirrhosis can happen to anyone but is more prevalent in alcoholics.

But because her liver could not process the drug, when they then gave here a second shot to ease her pain, the coma deepened and the end was eminent.

One of us kids, usually two together, would spend every minute with Mother in her room, making sure she was comfortable and trying to soothe her if we could. One night she became really bad; we thought she would die that night but she didn't. All the kids living in the area were called to her bedside to sit with her. That was the custom then. If you had a loved one dying, you shared the journey as far as you could.

Sometime in the wee hours of the next morning we were still gathered in the room when Mother appeared to come out of the coma and asked for me to come to her bedside. I went to her and she put her arms around me, kissed me on the cheek and told me she loved me.

She then lapsed back into the coma for a short while. Each time she became cognizant again she would ask for another child to come to her bedside and again she would repeat her message.

Sylvia was the final child called that morning. Mother gave her the same message as she had the rest of us. Then she looked at Sylvia, surprise evident on her face, and said, "I see him, I see him." Sylvia asked Mother whom she saw and she distinctly said, "Jesus." Sylvia told her if she truly saw Jesus to hug him too. Mother reached her arms up as though hugging someone and clasped her arms to her chest. Her message was a real as anything could ever be. Anyone doubting there is life after death should have been in that room with us.

When she was through hugging Jesus she looked around and asked for our brother Roy. Roy was not there that night. He had left a day or so before that to return to his home in Florida after spending a week at her bedside. We explained to mother that he had had to leave. She nodded her head to acknowledge she understood and then asked for our oldest brother, Palmer.

Palmer lived in New Jersey but had been called that night and was flying into the Indianapolis Airport. We explained his absence and she went into the coma again.

The next day one of us picked Palmer up and brought him to her bedside. As soon as he walked into the room and said, "Hi Mother," she woke again. Smiling at him she called him nearer and spoke to him the same message of love. Then she went back into a deep coma and after a month or so she died, having never awakened again.

She and Dad, who had been so close, were finally parted for good. Jimmy and I, along with Dad's brother, Pat, went to the nursing home to tell Dad Mother had died. We had to place him in the home so we could deal with Mother's illness and final moments. Even though Dad was heavily sedated, he understood and cried.

His own death four years later would be almost as traumatic, but not quite as dramatic. By his actions and expressions we knew he too was now in a better place.

The deaths of the others, my friend who committed suicide and my sisters-in-law who died of cancer and then our brother-in-law affected all of us, but not so much as Mother's death.

The death of this indomitable woman from the mountains of Eastern Kentucky left a hole in the hearts of everyone who knew her, but she left a legacy of goodness and kindness that can never be doubted. Her teachings affected not just her peers, but her children and their children and their children.

Today most of our own children and grandchildren live on with the knowledge imparted to their parents and grandparents by this one very special woman from the hills. May she rest in peace forever.

If there is anything I have said in this book that offends anyone I apologize. I have tried to portray the members of our family fairly. I hope you have enjoyed reading the words I have been called upon to write.

The following is the poem I had to write when our niece Misty Jane Day died. I hope you understand more about why I was forced to write it after reading the foregoing book.

Misty Jane

Hi Daddy, Hi Mommy,
It's me, Misty Jane
I just got up here today.
While your head was turned,
I just slipped away.

Two angels came and
Each took a hand.
They brought me up here
To play in their band.

Boy, it sure is pretty today,
The sun is shining.
And every cloud in the sky
Has its own silver lining.

Here is my halo,
Look! Can you see my wings?
I just think they are the
Most wondrous things.

I can fly, up in the air
Like a butterfly.
Or lie back on a cloud
And gaze at the sky.

And Mama its true,
The story they told.
The streets up here are
All paved with gold.

My mind is sound
My body is whole
But, I can see you crying,
Far, far below.

Don't cry for me Mama,
Don't weep for me Dad.
Be happy for me,
There's no reason to be sad.

I see Grandma and Grandpa,
And others we knew
I think I'll hang out with them
While I wait for you.

The music is heavenly,
The choir is divine.
I know I will have
A Splendiferous time.

Bye Daddy, By Mama,
And all of my kin.
May the Good Lord bless and keep you,
'Til we meet again.

Poem written by Misty Jane's Aunt
Helen the day after Misty Jane died on
October 16, 2001

Farewell

I would like to leave you now with the following poem that I wrote a few years back while I was recovering from the awful sickness I had in 1993. I tried to include as many of my happy, warm, fuzzy memories from childhood as I could remember. When I perform this poem for others I like to sing the first stanza of the song "Precious Memories", read the poem, and then sing the last stanza of the old familiar song.

My recovery period was a very serious writing period for me. It gave me what I and others who knew me considered a great gift of putting words together. It was written while I was beginning to formulate the idea for this book. This talent occurred when I was able to rise from my bed each morning. Every day was a new gift for me. I would arise, shake up the big box of words that I had in my brain, touch my fingertips to my keyboard and let the words flow out. It was the same box of words each day I woke up, but when the words went swirling together, they formed a different story or poem or song.

Some people ask me where I get my ideas for stories, poems and songs. I have to admit I do not know but when called upon to do so I must do what my brain and heart tells me to do or I will never get any rest until I do. My most creative moments occur when another person has touched my heart in some way.

Precious Memories Recitation

Yes, precious memories
Of days long ago.
The days of our childhood
Just wait to be told.

Feed sack dresses and pinafores
Big wide sashes, flour sack drawers.
Be-ribboned curls

On three little girls.
Homemade jelly and apple pie
Biscuits so fluffy they'd nearly fly.
4-H fairs, Christmas plays, blue skies
The sound of the band on the 4th of July

Bacon and eggs, sugar cured ham
Cornbread spread with blackberry jam.
A new-born calf, the old swimming hole
The heavenly scent of an old-fashioned rose.

Rides in the car, mother and dad singing
Sunday morning, church bells ringing.
Children laughing, hot summer days,
The sweet smell of new-mown hay.

The morning prayer, the golden rule
Walking barefoot to a 2-room school.
Taking up class at the sound of the bell,
Your own drinking glass, water drawn from a well.

Cold buttermilk, hot gingerbread men
A dog named Rover, a setting hen.
Squealing pigs, a four-leaf clover
Kids playing "Annie Over".

Golden grain, sweet corn in silk
Sauntering to the barn to milk.
Splashing in puddles after it rained
Shelling walnuts and getting stained.

Overnight company
Kids sleeping on the floor.
Wading the creek
And so much more.

Yes, Precious memories
Our food for the soul
They mean more to me
Than a pot full of gold.

Written by Helen Ayers
©11-19-98

The End or is it Just the Beginning?

Frank Fisher drew this picture for me.

About The Author

Mrs. Ayers is a retired self-educated newspaper journalist. She spent twenty-one years writing for and managing a weekly newspaper in central Indiana. She won many state and national press awards along the way for her stories. In her early years she worked as an executive secretary and computer programmer. In 1972, having decided to become a journalist, she quit her secretary job and set out to become a writer. Having a good editor helped her immensely and eight days after starting with the newspaper she was named its General Manager. One of her projects involved writing longer stories about people she knew who had died that week. These "Send Offs" became so popular that one older gentlemen asked her repeatedly to write his send off before he died so he could read what she had to say about him. She now lives in beautiful southern Brown County, Indiana with her husband, Mickey, and three little dogs. They have two sons and two grandchildren. She still loves to write stories and interview subjects.

www.ingramcontent.com/pod-product-compliance
Lightning Source LLC
Chambersburg PA
CBHW032111071025
33723CB00033B/211